O'NEILL FOR THE DEFENSE

A NOVEL

BY

CARL K. OSBORNE

Copyright 2017
Carl K. Osborne
All Rights Reserved

THIS IS A WORK OF FICTION.
ALL NAMES, PLACES, CHARACTERS, AND INCIDENTS, ARE ENTIRELY IMAGINARY AND ANY RESEMBLANCE TO ACTUAL EVENTS OR TO PERSONS LIVING OR DEAD, IS COINCIDENTAL.

ACKNOWLEDGEMENTS

I want to acknowledge the patience and creativity of my friend and editor Jamie Bailey, who made sense of my words and my wife, Janice who was always there to encourage me to keep going.

DEDICATION

I DEDICATE THIS BOOK TO THE Memory of

MARIO SANTOS

A young man who will always be in my thoughts.

ABOUT THE AUTHOR

Carl K. Osborne is a successful trial lawyer for the past fifty years in the field of criminal law. He grew up in a family involved in the entertainment industry in Hollywood. He was a member of the 1984 Olympic Advisory Board and started writing as a hobby over twenty years ago.

This book is number seven on his list of published novels and a sequel to "O'Neill's Law" published in 2016. His other books were "Out of Bounds", published in 2001 followed by "Supernotes" (2010), a book of "Short Stories" (2013), "Retribution" (2014), and "Backfired" (2015).

1

It was six long months since Devin O'Neill walked out of his office. He had replaced his cell phone with the newest iPhone available within two days of throwing it out his car window. His cell phone was, and had always been, a vital part of his life... almost like breathing. Summer was quickly approaching and he was calmer, his mind clearer and yet, he seemed to always be walking barefoot on an ant hill. His psychologist had suggested that he return to work; she thought he was ready. And although he was mostly enjoying his stress-free life, he had already started to contemplate the move. He could tell his family was getting antsy - *he always seemed to be around.*

He had been working out daily and it showed, he was running 25 miles a week. He felt physically strong however, his psychological health was far behind. He felt anxious with the thought of returning to work and he knew that his confidence really needed a boost. It was clear that everyone felt that way and that's why he was being pressed to return to his professional life. *They liked him being around at home but they would like him a lot more if he was back at work!* His wife had already secretly met with his law partners who were greatly encouraged about the possibility of his return.

Being on perpetual vacation made him feel like half a man; he was anxious to get the juices flowing again. He had recurring dreams about being in the courtroom, finding ways to beat the odds. The dreams made him smile, even as he slept. Then he would wake up in the morning with little or nothing to do except his workout routine, his kids were at school, his wife was busy creating and using her artistic skills in her art studio. It was time.

2

A couple of days earlier he had received a telephone call from one of his close friends, Beverly Silver. She asked him to have lunch with her. She needed some help concerning one of her friends who'd had a horrific run-in with the law. Devin was happy to get out of the house and away from his boring routine, so he agreed to meet the following day at Factor's Deli in Beverly Hills where, over pastrami sandwiches, she unfolded her story.

Beverly had grown up in the San Diego area where her family still lives; they were neighbors and close friends with the Tanners, who had a son, Jerry. He and Beverly were about the same age and grew up as close friends, even attending the same high school. When it was time to go to college she went to USC, Jerry went to UC Santa Barbara. They had stayed in contact with one another during their college years. After graduation, she married Conrad, whom she met at school, and they soon set off to become famous movie screenwriters. Jerry became a high school teacher and returned to San Diego where he got a job at a private boy's school, teaching junior-high school age boys. Having gone in different directions with their careers during this time, her relationship with Jerry had drifted apart.

About six years ago, her mother had called and said that she had just read in the local San Diego newspaper that Jerry had been arrested and was being charged with sexually molesting some of his students. By now Beverly was visibly distressed as she continued, "Devin, I couldn't believe my ears! That was so far out of character for him it didn't even make sense. It must be a mistake! I immediately called Jerry's brother, Mitchell, who is a practicing attorney living in Northern California. He verified the news that Jerry had, indeed, been arrested and charged."

She took a quick sip of her iced tea and wiped her eyes, now becoming clouded with tears. "I was very upset and immediately drove to San Diego and met with his parents and brother, who had flown down from San Francisco. Jerry was in jail with a million-dollar bail hanging over his head. Mitchell explained that he was in the process of hiring a local lawyer to represent him and post bail. That afternoon we all went down to the county jail to visit Jerry. He looked pathetic sitting behind the glass window in an orange jumpsuit. Mitchell and Jerry talked over the phone while his parents and I stood by. Mitchell told him not to say anything that they were working on getting him out."

The look on her face had changed from emotionally spent to vivid anger. "Fast forward about a year and a half later, guess what? He went to trial and was found guilty on all charges! I sat in disbelief through the entire two weeks of trial. I couldn't believe how his lawyers sucked; he had two lawyers. I called them Tweedle Dee and Tweedle Dumb. When it was over, the judge sentenced Jerry to 15 years to life. The case was immediately appealed and the family found another attorney to handle the appellate process. Unbeknownst to them, this lawyer had a serious drug problem and almost missed the filing deadline for the appeal."

"Unfortunately," she continued, "his conviction was upheld, so the family appealed to the California Supreme Court and they have just received the bad news. The family is inconsolable. They don't know what to do. Jerry is in Folsom State prison. I swear that he is innocent."

"They should have hired you from the beginning, Devin, but I didn't have a say. I have now insisted that, if there is any chance of getting him a new trial, they must hire you!"

Devin said, "Beverly, you know that I'm presently on a timeout from work, right?"

Beverly responded, "I know, but there is no one else except you that can get this done. His family and his friends have put together a defense fund of approximately $250,000 and it's yours if there's anything you can do. What do you think?"

"As I see it, there's only one remedy left to get him a new trial and that's by way of a writ of habeas corpus, and the chances of that happening are about one in a million."

"I like those odds, Devin. Please! Please say you'll do it for me?" Beverly responded. This put Devin on the spot he was not an appellate attorney. He knew nothing about the case. It would require him to read the trial transcripts, the appeal briefs and the court decisions. He'd have to look outside of the record to find some new evidence or show that his lawyers did such a bad job that the trial was unfair. To complicate matters more, he did not like to involve himself with friends or family, that's always a bad combination. It usually dooms the friendship, he reminded himself. But at this point, Beverly was not taking no for an answer.

Devin explained that there were strict time limitations on filing writs. "Do you know when the California Supreme Court's decision was handed down?"

"I don't know exactly, but it's been within the last couple of weeks."

"I'm not promising anything here, but how fast could you get me the files?" Beverly replied within the week.

"Who was his appellate lawyer?" Beverly didn't know. He took a small bite of his sandwich and began slowly explaining what he was willing to do.

"This is how it's going to work. I will review the court records to see if there's anything there that I can hang my hat on. Once I get the files, I'll need at least two weeks to do my review. I will require an initial deposit of $25,000 to get the work started. If I feel there's hope for pursuing and moving forward with the case, I will apply that money towards the writ. My office personnel will be assisting me. But remember, I'm making no promises, Bev. I don't want this to interfere with our friendship."

Beverly couldn't hide her relief and her excitement. "I understand. I have no expectations but I know if there's a way, you'll make it happen! Thanks so much for your willingness to work for this innocent man and his family, Devin. I have never, and would never, let anything interfere with our friendship, promise."

3

The next morning Devin called Michelle at the office; they had not spoken for nearly six months. He explained to her that he was thinking of coming back to work. Michelle started to cry, telling him through her tears, that she'd been waiting for this day to happen, it was long overdue. He instructed her to call a meeting of the partners as soon as possible and to include Ted and Ray, also.

Within a few minutes of hanging up, she called back with all the needed information. "How about tomorrow at noon? I'll order lunch in for everyone." And just that easily, Devin was back. Done.

That evening he told his wife that he was returning to work. She smiled from ear-to-ear, holding his face in her hands, looking at the obvious joy in his eyes. "Go for it my dear husband. The world will be a better place with you directing traffic." He hugged her, not wanting to let go, confirming what he already knew – *she was the best thing that ever happened to him.*

After telling the kids the news, hearing them all cheer in unison, Devin laughed as he realized just how happy they were to get him out of the house. That night after a couple of hits on a joint and some of the best sex that he'd had in a while, he slept with a calm smile on his face.

He was up at six, took a three-mile run, charged his phone and laptop and headed for the office. It seemed that the entire day was designed to welcome him back. The sky was a clear, piercing blue with white puffy clouds everywhere, and the traffic was almost non-existent. The trip to his old office haunts was familiar, and within fifteen minutes he pulled into the building parking lot where he was greeted at the gate by Carlos. "Mr.O! How nice to see you! Where have you been?" Devin just smiled. It's a new day, a new life. He was ready and raring to go.

Up the elevator to the penthouse, he walked briskly through the double doors bearing his name, through the reception area and into the office. It was a party everyone was in the bullpen area. There were loud cheers welcome home balloons and banners everywhere. He held his breath for a second and realized - he was home! He felt like a million as he realized how much he had missed this part of his life. He understood, for the first time, how much he had needed the break... and his feelings about his return today really proved it.

Once the hugs and kisses and handshakes were over, Devin walked into the conference room where there was an amazingly large deli spread for everybody. When the din finally settled down, the afternoon was all business. In an extraordinarily smooth process, he was brought up to date on the current cases and the financial condition of the firm. He congratulated and thanked everyone for the great job they had done in his absence. He had refused any compensation during his absence but, unbeknownst to him, his partners had put his share of the profits away and presented him with a check for $150,000. He said 'no' they said 'yes, end of story' and they won the debate. Humbled at the welcome back reception by everyone, he knew it was time to get back to work before he got sentimental. He thanked everyone and asked Ted, Ray and Michelle to accompany him to his office. No trepidations, no doubts, he shook off the rust and settled into the life he'd been missing.

Once settled, Devin started to explain his conversation with Ms. Silver, saying she was a close, personal, friend; that she had pleaded with him to investigate the conviction of one of her friends for molesting young boys, his students. The appeals process had run its course, but she still insists that he is innocent and feels there was a serious miscarriage of justice.

Devin continued, "I don't like the idea, particularly because of our friendship, however, I want you to know that I agreed. I said okay, we'll work on it. The defendant's family and friends have raised over $250,000 for his defense, and she gave me a check for $25,000.00 to review the record of the case."

Without further comment, he reached into his briefcase and handed Michelle the check asking her to please deposit it in the firm's account. "The client's name is Jerry Tanner. The case originated in San Diego County. I don't have a lot of information other than he was a schoolteacher and was convicted after a jury trial and sentenced to 15 years to life. The appeals were lost all the way through to the California Supreme Court. That decision is only a couple of weeks old. I've obtained a case number and the name of the appellate attorney."

He gave Michelle instructions to prepare a retainer agreement for the client's parents' signature and a letter to Paul Cross, the appellate attorney, requesting all the files. He asked Ray to arrange to get the files and pleadings from him as soon as possible. "My friend is convinced that the trial attorneys did a terrible job. Of course, that may be hard to prove since I'm sure her mind is tainted because of her friendship with the defendant."

Walking over to Ted, he continued. "Ted, you are my eyes and ears when it comes to appeals. I readily admit that it's a specialty I'm not as well-versed in as you are, so if you have the time, could you go up to Folsom for an interview with the client? Your insight is extremely important. In the meantime, I will give the trial lawyers a call and get their take on how the case went."

Everyone was on board with their tasks. Devin was back in the mix as if he'd never left. Things were in motion. Once the conversation about the Tanner case was finished, Ted and Ray asked if Devin was ready to get up to date on all their current cases. Asking to be brought in slowly, Devin began his trek back to the pulse of the firm, the important familiarization process. It was after 5 PM when they had finally finished. Devin thanked them for their patience and for having it all covered, assuring them he'd jump in and get his feet wet with the Tanner case.

4

It was only five days back to work and everyone was performing at 100%. Devin was extremely proud of how his team worked together. They gathered in the conference room with the trial transcripts, the record on the appeals, along with the court's rulings. Still feeling a bit like the Grand Master, Ted had just returned from his visit with Jerry Tanner at the prison. He started off by using the notes that he had taken during their meeting. In his opinion, there was a real possibility that the client could just be innocent. *Jerry had told him that he was 32, single, and engaged to be married at the time of his arrest. That he had graduated UC Santa Barbara with honors and that he was also captain of the debate team. After graduation, he had returned to San Diego with his teaching credentials in hand and got a job as a math teacher and part-time coach with Canyon Academy, a private prep school for boys through the ninth grade, in the San Diego area. He had been a teacher there for five years when he* was accused of sexually molesting his male students. He claimed it was total bullshit; it was just horse-play with his kids in the classroom. His story is very believable. He explained that sometimes after class he would wrestle with some of the boys in the classroom, always in front for everyone to see; that sometimes he would pick them up by the beltline of their pants and throw them about. It was just a Laugh, everyone had fun. It was never sexual. This kind of activity went on for years, nobody thought anything about it.

One day a substitute teacher saw him throwing some of the boys around and grabbing them by the pants, picking them up. She reported it to the principal, explaining that she saw Jerry put his hands down the front of the pants of a couple of his students, that she felt that it was her obligation to report the incident, demanding that the principle make a report to the authorities and if she didn't, she would.

It turns out that the principal, Andrea Jones, was fully aware of Jerry's behavior and had told him many times to cool it; that it was not something a teacher should be doing. But in her mind, it was harmless and the kids liked it and looked up to him like a big brother. She knew that this complaint could cause serious harm to Jerry, as well as the school, if the authorities were brought in. She told the teacher that she would report her observations. However, thinking the substitute teacher had only a couple of days left in her schedule, she decided to hold off and maybe just forget the conversation. That afternoon, Mrs. Jones explained the situation and her dilemma to Jerry and told him to immediately stop his horse-play, that other people were getting the wrong idea. Jerry agreed to do so, but thought it was completely harmless, so how could anyone believe otherwise. Mrs. Jones told him not to be so naïve, that there were many people out there on a witch hunt.

The next couple of days, everything seemed to be going smoothly until Friday afternoon, when a couple of San

Diego police detectives, along with a woman from Child Protective Services, showed up in the principal's office. Mary Fox, the substitute teacher, had filed a formal complaint with her affidavit under penalty of perjury, stating her observations of Tanner's conduct; including that she had reported the incident to the school principal. This put Mrs. Jones on the defensive since she had not reported the incident to the authorities. She told them that she was in the process of making a report, but with an abundance of caution, was conducting her own investigation, including interviews with the children involved so she could present a complete picture when done. The cat was out of the bag! She had lost total control of the situation. She was told to suspend the teacher pending their investigation, and requested a list of his students, which she reluctantly gave them.

Over the next two weeks they conducted interviews with each child after notifying their parents. Alarm bells went off. The local newspapers got wind of the investigation and it snowballed into an avalanche. At first the boys all thought the whole thing was funny but as it went on, the psychologists who did the interviews were putting false ideas into their heads. By the time the authorities had finished, eight boys acknowledged that their teacher had touched their genitals, making them feel uncomfortable. The parents were in an uproar. Many of them removed their children from the school. Civil lawsuits started being filed, claiming the school was aware of what was going on and did nothing to stop it. The pressure was on and that's when Jerry was arrested and charged.

Ted had assessed Jerry's explanations and remarked that the physical contact with his students had always taken place in the classroom in front of other students, and that it was totally inconsistent with any sexual molestation cases that he had ever heard of. Devin asked if he was ever examined by a psychologist with a specialty in pedophilia. Ted said he wasn't aware of any such examination.

"To your knowledge, did he ever take a polygraph exam?" Not to his knowledge, was Ted's response. Devin went on to update everyone on his inability to speak to the trial counsel yet, because one of them was now a sitting Superior Court Judge out of county, and his co-counsel was away on vacation.

Ray jumped into the conversation stating that he had read the preliminary hearing transcript and the trial transcript and that a few things stood out. *First, in the original complaint there were eight counts charged representing the eight alleged victims. Each boy testified at the preliminary hearing; seven of the boys' testimony was rather weak, however, one boy, Franklin Sloan, was over the top with his. Thus, Tanner was held to answer on all counts, but here's the interesting thing, when the information was filed, it only included seven counts.*

Franklin Sloan was the oldest boy of the group and was the prosecution's best witness in testifying about Jerry's sexual advances towards him, but that count was *dropped. Ask yourself, why drop **his case?** It was their strongest. That raised a red flag for me. The trial itself was strange, from a defense point of view. The prosecution put on a basic prima facie case, cut and dry. The defendant did not testify; I question that. Also, there were no defense expert's witnesses. Why not? The defense's main thrust was to try to impeach the children, not a good idea, from my point. They put on many character witnesses to say what a good person Tanner was; what was the use of that? Some people think Hitler was a good person, for God's sake. He needed to testify, himself. I do question why the defense did not do more? Usually, in these types of cases, it's important to show how the children can be manipulated by the psychologists and the pressure from their families. None of this was done, and the jury still took five days to reach their decision. The appellate briefs didn't point to any trial errors, relying on the insufficiency of the evidence. It appears that the court's decision was a foregone conclusion. The prosecution witnesses* *established that the defendant touched the boys' genitals when he would put his hand down the front of their pants; what else could they conclude without hearing from the defendant? It's very apparent that the lawyers just took his money.*

Devin said, "This is a good start but we're going to need a lot more for any real chance of success. I'll talk with the trial attorneys maybe they will open some doors. "

5

That night Devin took home the appellate briefs and the court's opinions to review. After four hours of reading the materials, he concluded the lawyers failed in providing an adequate defense. It was an easy win for the prosecution. The defense lawyers could get off the hook by explaining that the way they presented their defense was a trial tactic. Devin knew that unless there were facts outside of the record it would be hopeless. The hope was that his interviews with trial counsel might give him an opening. He had left his cell phone number with Stephen Knowles' secretary, asking to have him return the call as soon as possible because he needed his help deciding whether to proceed with a writ on behalf of Tanner.

While driving to the office, Devin's phone rang. He put it on speaker, it was Knowles. Devin quickly explained that he had called because time was of the essence, every day was a loss until he could file the writ.

Knowles said, "I feel bad about Jerry. I believed in his innocence."

"Listen, I've read parts of the record, I'd like to ask you some questions. I don't want to put you on the spot, but as we know, the question of competency of counsel is grounds for a new trial."

"I know. I'm willing to fall on my sword."

"Good. I'm in my car now, so can I call you back within the next half hour?"

Knowles said, "I'll be waiting," and hung up.

Devin knew he needed to be somewhat delicate so as not to scare Knowles by making accusations. He would play it by ear and let the conversation take its course. Once at the office, he took his seat at his desk, with pen and yellow pad in hand, he was ready to make the call. The first thing he did to disarm him was to explain who he was, that he had been asked by a friend to consider reviewing Tanner's case, strictly as a favor, since the California

Supreme Court had rejected Tanner's appeal. He asked Knowles if he would mind answering a few questions. Knowles said "No, please ask away."

Devin began, "I understand you represented Jerry from the get-go, from the original arraignment through the sentencing phase, correct?"

"Yes, that's the time frame."

"Were you the lead attorney for the case?"

Knowles cleared his throat, "Gregory Thompson was, but I did a great deal of the work in preparing the case for trial. Did you know that he was appointed to the bench right after the trial? He's now a sitting judge in Imperial County."

"No, I didn't. Where is that?"

Knowles sounded a bit sarcastic, "Somewhere out in the boondocks, not a plum assignment."

"Interesting. So, what was the theme of your defense, your game plan, in other words?" Devin continued.

Knowles replied, "We felt that the boys were coached into believing that the activity was of a sexual nature, so we approached the case hoping to expose them."

"How were you going to do that?"

"By having an aggressive cross-examination, our goal was to break them down."

Devin asked if any of them had a history of lying or misbehavior, anything like that. Knowles replied, not really.

"Did you employ an investigator to delve into their family backgrounds?"

"Yes, we did, and found that they all came from middle-class, Catholic backgrounds; six of the eight were Hispanic."

"Can you tell me about Franklin Sloan? I understand that he testified at Tanner's prelim and in reading the transcript, he seems to be the prosecution's star witness?"

Knowles acknowledged that he had been. He explained, "We learned through our investigators, from some of the children who were not part of the case, and from some of the teaching staff that he was kind of rebellious, a 'smart ass,' as some of his teachers described him. They said he was looked up to by the other boys and that sometimes Tanner had to put him in his place by embarrassing him in front of them. For example, one day during the horseplay Tanner picked him up by the back of his pants, turned him upside down and put him headfirst into a trash can, causing the other kids to laugh. Needless to say, he was not a happy camper."

"The record reflects that the count involving Sloan was dropped by the people. My question is why? He was a strong witness."

"I know. When we asked the DA why, their answer was that they thought their case was cleaner without him."

"Did you ever check into their reasoning or rationale for such a decision?"

"No. The DA, Sonja Levin, was a straight-shooter so we just took her word for it."

"Did you or your investigators ever interview Sloan?"

"We tried but we were stonewalled by Children's Protective Services and his parents."

"Did you think that was strange?"

"Of course, we did, but what could we do? Our hands were tied."

"Did your investigator interview any of the other boys or their parents?"

Again, Knowles replied that they had been told by the DA and the investigating officers they did not have to speak to us and that ended that.

"Do you know where Sloan is now? He must be over 18 years old."

Knowles replied, "No clue. After the sentencing, we turned our files over to Tanner's appellate attorneys."

Shifting gears, Devin asked evenly, "Can you tell me why Jerry did not testify in his own defense?"

"We thought it would be better if he did not. We all know that the touching occurred; that was never the issue. It was his intent with the horse- playing, and frankly, we thought he would be vulnerable on cross examination. We preferred not to chance it."

"Did he have any baggage in his background?"

"None that I know of."

"I understand that he was highly educated and, in fact, was the captain of his college debate team; didn't you think he could handle himself?"

Knowles remarked that being a witness, accused of these types of crimes carried with it a great deal of pressure, far greater than anything he'd been used to. "We just didn't think he was up to the task, so that's how we called it."

"Did he want to testify?"

"Yes, but we put our foot down, deciding it was in his best interest."

Afraid of what the answer might be to his next question, Devin continued, "Did you explain to him that even if you didn't want him up on the stand, it was his decision, not yours?"

Sounding a bit agitated, Knowles replied, "Not directly. He was, as you said, a highly-educated man who knew his rights!"

Devin dropped the subject and went a different direction with his questions, "Why no experts?"

The response was that it was ultimately his decision; Tanner was afraid of the results, so he said no.

"Did you explain to him that if the results were unfavorable they would just hit the trash can?"

"No, it never went that far. He just flatly said no."

"Did you do anything to try to impeach the boys' interviewing therapists?"

"We took a hard look at that but they had followed procedure. Our experts reviewed the interviews and, in their words, we were cautioned, "Don't go there, you'll only reinforce the boys' stories."

Pausing to take down the notes, Devin asked for the investigator's name and requested that he be given a heads-up that Devin would be calling. He ended the phone call with, "Thank you for being candid with me. I appreciate your time and I hope I can call you again if needed?" Knowles responded of course.

Devin sat there with his pile of notes, thinking there must be a lot more under the surface. He buzzed Ted's office and asked if he could come over, he wanted to run the conversation with Knowles by him.

After Devin's review of the conversation, Ted pointed out, "It looks like he left you an opening about Tanner not testifying, don't you think?"

Devin nodded. "Absolutely, we need to get a definitive answer from the client about whether he was fully aware that it was his decision alone, not his lawyers', about whether to testify or not. There must have been many conversations about that. Knowles admitted he did not *specifically* advise him of that right; he danced around it." "His rationale about not wanting Tanner to testify was weak. He admits that the defendant was well-educated, with no baggage, and an excellent speaker; in fact, captain of his college debate team. But I really believe there's something he's not telling us."

Looking hard at his notes, he continued, "The court did not advise Tanner of his rights either, which they usually do. "Why not here? Why keep him off the stand? It's a small opening, so let's widen it."

"Also, I didn't like his explanation of why the DA dropped Sloan from the case. It was very convenient to say it was because the DA was 'beyond being honest', but we all know they want to win as badly as the defense. They just don't throw away their best witness. I really think something smells. We need to investigate further, we're still not ready or able to file any kind of writ."

He asked Ted if he would call the prison to speak with Tanner and ask about his reasoning for not testifying in court and for stonewalling his defense teams' request to hire experts. He also had Michelle make an appointment with Francis Wright, the defense investigator.

Later that afternoon Devin phoned Beverly and updated her on his progress, explaining that he would be in San Diego in two days to speak with the trial attorney's investigators. Moving fast now, he asked Ray to start preparing a bare-bones writ, using the California Public Defenders Association in Sacramento as a contact, if he needed some samples of successful writs as a guideline. They had all the best pleadings, motions and writs available. This was what he used to do when researching cases requiring successful writs, saving a lot of time and guesswork. The county court clerk's office could provide copies of the files; it was always smart to use other successful attorneys' work, if possible. Why reinvent the wheel? Ray was pleased. Great idea!

6

Devin arrived at a two-story, white brick building across from Balboa Park near the San Diego Zoo. It was 10 AM. He had left LA at seven. Traffic was terrible as usual, but he did make good time. He did not want to be late for his meeting with Francis Wright. He walked briskly to the offices located on the ground floor.

As Devin entered through the front door, he was greeted by Mr. Wright *(so his gold name badge showed)*. A tall man with white hair, blue eyes and a white, bushy mustache, Devin thought he must be in his late 60's. He looked dapper, wearing a dark blue suit with yellow suspenders. He invited Devin into a conference room where a *'younger'* Francis Wright was seated. The real Francis introduced him as his son, Wayne. After the introductions and some brief, polite conversation, Devin explained his purpose for the meeting.

"I have a two-fold agenda today, gentlemen. First, I need to learn as much as I can about the Tanner case and, secondly, I'd like to retain your services going forward. You have an excellent reputation as investigators and, being local, you know more about the case than anyone I can think of."

Francis started by explaining that he was retired FBI and that his son had gone through law school, then decided he didn't want to be a lawyer, so had joined the San Diego Sheriff's Department and became a homicide detective. "When I retired and started my own investigation firm, he joined me. One of the plusses was that he spoke Spanish, and that helped a lot."

Devin began the process by asking to be filled in on their role with the Tanner investigation.

Francis shared the history of his almost ten-year old firm and their work with many of the high-profile law firms in the area.

"One day a local attorney, Stephen Knowles, came to my office and told me that he was representing a teacher charged in multiple counts of sexually molesting his students; that he needed background checks on the victims and their families. Once we agreed to participate, he provided us with the police reports. Lucky for us, Wayne was acquainted with one of the investigators, Paul Cano, who he'd worked with on a couple of murder investigations."

At this point, Wayne jumped into the conversation explaining that he had called Cano, who agreed to sit down with him over a couple of beers to discuss his opinions about the case. *"He told me that he was not comfortable about it from the beginning. The kids were all saying the right things, however, he recognized that the ADA in charge of the case was very aggressive and wanted to use this case to make a name for herself. He told me that he was never allowed to interview any of the boys except in the presence of the ADA and/or Child Protective Services officer, Phyllis Marks, even though he had handled* many of these types of cases before and was very experienced."

"The way this investigation was being handled was all wrong, but he said nothing. He had searched the defendant's residence, his computers; nothing turned up. The computers were clean. The neighbors, other teachers and school officials all had praise for him."

He continued, "The way the alleged sexual activity went down was odd. Cano explained that all the kids came from Spanish-speaking families, except for two. They were all middle-class, blue-collar workers. The kids were on a special grant program, that's how they were able to attend such an expensive, respected private school. He provided me with all the families' contact information. After that meeting, I made attempts to speak with each of the students and their families, but only one would speak to me, Tony Villa. I met with him and his mom, Rosa, at their apartment. She was nervous and seemed hesitant to speak with me, saying that she was supposed to call the social worker or the DA if anyone tried to talk to her or her son about the case. I told her if she wanted to call, to go ahead, but she said no. By the way, our conversation was in Spanish."

"I asked her how her son was doing? She surprised me by saying that he had felt pressured. I asked her how? She explained that the police and the counselors asked him to say things that weren't true, but he was afraid to say anything. He liked Mr. Tanner, but he had to do what they said or he wouldn't get any money for school, and they were poor. I asked who had told him that? He said that one of the guys said that he would ruin everything if he didn't go along. I asked if I could record his statement. He said no, they were afraid, then they asked me to leave. All the other families refused to speak to me at all."

We both attended the preliminary hearing and listened to each of the boys' testimony, I thought it was well rehearsed. It was obvious to me which boy was putting on the pressure, it was Franklin Sloan. Later, when I *heard that the prosecution dropped the charges on his count by not including it in the information, I told the attorneys they needed to inquire why the DA had dropped that case? I thought something was up, that they might be aware of what he was orchestrating and, if he stayed in, he could blow up their case."*

"After the preliminary, I attempted to interview Sloan but his father flatly refused, only to say that they were suing the school and Tanner for millions, and that if I continued to attempt to talk to his son, he would call the police and the DA, and say I was trying to intimidate them, so we dropped it."

"At the trial, one of the things that I noticed was that all the boys and their parents were together in the same waiting room while waiting to testify. I advised Knowles about it, making it clear that I knew witnesses were usually kept apart so as not to discuss their testimony. Knowles told me that they were being supervised, so there was no problem. I asked who was supervising? He said Phyllis

Marks, the social worker. To me it was like letting the fox watch over the chicken house. Anyway, it wasn't my call, after the verdict I felt numb, but I moved on."

Devin was stunned by all he'd heard. "All the boys must by adults by now, right? Do you think you could track them down and attempt to re-interview them? It might really help."

Francis sat up straight in his chair and looking at Wayne for confirmation, said, "It would be my pleasure to help! I never liked the way the case went down, maybe we can do some good. How do we get started?"

"Please e-mail me your retainer right away. By the way, what is your hourly fee?"?

Francis replied, "$150 an hour plus travel expenses. I require a $10,000 deposit against hours to start."

As all three got to their feet, Devin shook hands and said, "Ok, gentlemen. Let's get started. I need copies of all investigative reports as soon as possible." Francis said, done!

The meeting had lasted five hours, it was almost three o'clock. Devin called Beverly, who was visiting her mother in Rancho Santa Fe. He stopped by on his way back to LA and reported in over a glass of wine.

7

Devin, Ted, and Ray met early the following day. They had to decide whether they should go forward or pass. The question was, did they have enough to file a writ or should they wait and see what Francis Wright came up with? The statute was running and time was of the essence; if they filed now, it would stay the statute.

Ted had already prepared a declaration for Jerry to sign, clearly establishing that he was never informed of his right to make the decision to testify, so he believed they had enough to file now. "If we can get Knowles to acknowledge that as his counsel, he failed to advise him, I think that would be grounds to get the writ granted on that issue alone. And if the investigation comes up with more, we can move to amend."

Devin added that he believed there was still a lot that could be uncovered, which would add strength to the writ. Ray worried that it could take months and if they waited and nothing materialized, they would have wasted all that time. Ted agreed and suggested they should ask the client.

Devin replied, 'Okay, I'll handle that. I'm sure Tanner will tell us to go forward. Why wouldn't he? Anything's better than just sitting in jail with no hope, right?"

"Let's get the family in here quickly and explain all the options, let them discuss the matter among themselves, and make a decision," Ted suggested.

"Great! I'll delay the investigator for a week and in the meantime, I'll draft a declaration for Knowles to sign. I sure as hell hope he cooperates."

Devin asked Ted to get Tanner's signature on his declaration and for Ray to leave a copy of the draft of the writ on his desk and a copy for Ted's review. He knew this was a long shot, at best, but if nothing was done, Tanner wouldn't see the outside of his cell for another fifteen years. What an amazing injustice! That afternoon he called Beverly and asked her to gather the *'powers that be'* for a meeting in his office, as soon as possible. *They were on a roll and it was decision time.*

Three days later, Devin, Ted and Ray were seated around the conference table with Beverly, Jerry's mother and father and his brother. After a brief but thorough explanation, all their questions were answered. Devin had received the signed declaration by Knowles, where he admitted, in essence, that he never advised Jerry of his right to testify, even in the face of his attorney's opposition. This failure was good grounds to get a new trial if they acted quickly. They understood the pressing issue of the statute of limitations on filing writs, as Laid down by the U.S. Congress; the longer they waited, the less time available for the process of going through various courts, both state and federal, required for a final decision.

"I believe there's a lot more behind-the-scenes information to uncover which could possibly give us additional grounds to make the petition even stronger, but that could take months. I don't believe we can afford to wait."

"Finally, it's important for you to know that this process is going to be expensive; the legal fees could easily run over a hundred thousand dollars. Plus, additional costs, including experts and investigative fees; these could run another $50,000 or so, and in the end, there is no way to guarantee that the court will see the case as we see it. The final decision is yours and Jerry's. We're asking that you consider it from all angles. Talk among yourselves and Jerry, ask any questions you may have while you deliberate the pros and cons... write down questions or concerns as you think of them and we'll answer everything we possibly can. It's not an easy decision to make because it's mired in raw emotion, proving potential injustice and, of course, the personal connections to your own family member. We'll give you your privacy." Then Devin, Ray and Ted left the room.

Forty-five minutes later Beverly came out of the conference room and asked Michelle to ask Devin to join them. When all three had returned, the questions went on for another fifteen minutes. Once everyone felt assured the questions were answered and dealt with, they all agreed to go forward. Beverly explained that they would speak with Jerry immediately and asked them to be prepared to move quickly. As they all left with hugs and handshakes, Devin reminded them, "Remember. No promises."

8

After receiving the green light, the Petition for the writ of habeas corpus was put together quickly. All three reviewed the rough draft provided by Ray, and after a few independent additions and deletions, the final revision was approved and ready to file. Although confident that they had done their best work for filing, Devin took one more precautionary step and, without telling anyone, drove out to Riverside to personally meet with Brent Romney, an experienced, highly respected criminal lawyer who had been in front of the California Supreme Court many times. Devin admired his work and wanted his opinion of the Petition. It passed muster!

The following day it was filed in Superior Court of San Diego, North District in Vista, where the original trial for Tanner was held. It was filed with the original trial judge, Lowell Brown, with copies to San Diego DA's Office and the California State Attorney General's Office. Now all they could do was wait, there was no time limit for the court to rule.

If you received a postcard in the mail, you lose. The procedural steps after that are to go to the California Court of Appeals; if you lose there, you go to the California Supreme Court. If you're in the losing spiral, you start all over in United States District Court. The final step is the Ninth Circuit Court. You can consider it *game over* if you lose there because it's known as the most liberal court in the nation. Devin had explained to the family that early losses were to be expected; that the case could easily wind up in the Ninth Circuit. *Close your eyes, cross your fingers, hold your breath...*

Four days Later Ray called Devin at home saying he was at the office early and that there was a notification from the court stating that Judge Brown had reassigned the Petition to Presiding Judge Dana Cole. *No postcard denial!* Devin was elated and immediately got on the phone to call his good friend, Dennis Fredrickson, who had practiced law in San Diego for many years and was familiar with the judges in Vista. He wanted to get a read on Cole. To Devin's surprise, Dennis told him that Cole was a good friend and considered to be a very liberal judge. Before becoming a judge, he was head of the ACLU in San Diego. *Another great sign!* Devin knew that writs like this had an extremely slim chance in the lower courts. *Should he start believing all the signs and hope that this could be the one in a lifetime?* He kept this information to himself, going about his business, hoping for the best, but preparing to step back into his old shoes, if need be. Just keep charging your batteries, you'll need them either way.

He lunched with a couple of his Chinese and Vietnamese connections from the past who had been instrumental in referring a lot of their communities' business to the firm. Having worked closely on a variety of cases, they were very loyal to Devin and had decided to hold off doing business with anyone else since he'd been gone. They were delighted that he was back and were anxious to rekindle old friendships.

Jackson Mo was the senior of the two, Lam was his Vietnamese partner. Over lunch, Jackson explained he'd just been contacted by one of his associates in Sacramento who wanted to refer what he considered a giant federal drug case. He told Devin, "I was about to turn him down but if you're back, it's yours, if you want it."

Devin was all smiles, asking for more information on the case.

"As far as I know the client is from San Francisco, charged with conspiracy to grow and distribute large quantities of marijuana. During the real estate market downturn, his group acquired approximately twenty single-family residences in the Sacramento area and converted them into marijuana grow houses with an annual crop exceeding a ton a year, according to the police reports. The DEA was the arresting agency and they indicated that the business was making millions."

All ears now, Devin asked, "When did the client get arrested?"

"I'm not sure. I'll call Jimmy Tang, he's my contact. Maybe we can meet tomorrow and get all the details for you."

"That's great, Jackson. Make it work. Looks like a big payday."

"Okay, boss. Just like old times, right?"

As they got up to leave, Lam said, "Devin we really missed you! I'll up put the word out that we are back in business." The old friends hugged and left their old hangout, NBC Seafood Restaurant. On his way from Monterey Park, Devin called Ray and told him they were back in business in the Chinese community.

Ray couldn't believe it. "Don't they say there's no rest for the wicked?" Devin laughed out loud.

9

Deep in thought as he gazed at the amazing view from his office window, the loud buzzer rudely interrupted. "I have a Mr. Wright on the phone. Shall I put it through?" Devin replied, yes.

It was Wayne, *Francis Jr.* "I'm at the apartment of Tony Villa. He wants to talk. I think you should be present to hear this. He has an unbelievable story, that if true, blows the Tanner conviction sky high."

Devin just sat there, listening. Wayne confirmed that Tony was a second-year student attending San Diego State, so his class and work schedules gave him a window of either Friday afternoon, or Saturday morning. He preferred this Saturday or next, because he wanted his mother to be a participant in the conversation.

Devin offered to make himself available when it worked best for them. After checking with Tony, this Saturday at 9:30 AM was confirmed for a meeting. Wayne assured Devin that a separate meeting with him was unnecessary because he wanted him to hear what Tony had to say, directly from his mouth.

"Don't keep me in suspense. Do I need to prepare for this in any way?" Devin asked. Wayne replied that he'd hear it all in two days, with that he hung up.

Devin still had heard nothing from the court about Tanner's Petition, it had been over a couple of weeks. He was confident they wouldn't be 'postcarded' at this late date. On Friday, he drove down to San Diego with his wife, he thought he would make a weekend of it. He booked two nights at Morgan's Run in Rancho Santa Fe, with a round of golf. She usually beat his ass but he didn't care, they always really enjoyed each other's company.

On Saturday morning, he arrived at the apartment building just east of downtown San Diego on the outskirts of San Diego State's campus. It looked like student housing. He approached apartment 2-D on the second floor and knocked on the door. Wayne opened the door and invited Devin in. As he entered the living room, there was no question it was home to a student; the messy room, empty beer cans, dirty dishes, books and papers all over the place. A young man in his early 20's was seated in what loosely looked like a couch, wearing a San Diego State T-shirt and gray shorts and no shoes. Wayne introduced Devin to Tony as he stood and shook Devin's hand and then sat down again. A minute went by when a short, plump woman in her early 50's came into the room. She had short black hair and was nicely dressed. Wayne introduced Rosa as Tony's mother, explaining that her English was quite limited. Shaking hands with Devin, she sat down next to her son.

Wayne started the conversation. "I spoke with Tony the other day and he allowed me to record that conversation, and he's agreed that whatever is said this morning can also be recorded." Rosa said something in Spanish. Wayne translated it into English.

"She said her son is a wonderful young man and wants to right a wrong. I'm behind him 100%". Devin thanked her on behalf of Jerry Tanner.

For the next two hours Devin sat there, absorbing Tony's words, wanting to remain a fly on the wall. The story went like this:

"When Tony started classes at Canyon Academy he was placed into a special group of boys, basically his own age. They all came from Spanish-speaking families, with Spanish as their first language, although all the students were English proficient. They all became a close-knit group because of their backgrounds, and Jerry Tanner became like a counselor and a friend to them, not just a teacher. They liked him and liked to horse-play with each other in the classroom or the gym. He would frequently pick them up and throw them about the room during the breaks from studying. It was great fun and everyone looked forward to just hanging out and goofing off. During the horse-play, he would sometimes grab us by the beltline and pick us up and twirl us around; this might happen a few times a week between classes."

Straightening up on the messy sofa with his mother sitting next to him, Tony continued. "There were a couple of kids in our class who thought they were better than us. They were white kids."

Wayne asked who. "*Sloan and a kid named Gray, they would hang together. Mr. Tanner included them in our games; they weren't bullies, but they made us feel like second-class citizens. It was obvious by their behavior towards us. Sometimes Mr. Tanner would pick them up by the pants and put them in a trash can, we kind of liked that it brought them back down to earth.*"

"*One day we were all called down to the principal's office, all twelve of us, including Sloan and Gray, where we were introduced to a couple of police officers and a woman from child services. They talked to all of us together for about thirty minutes explaining that they were there to investigate Mr. Tanner sexually assaulting us. I really didn't understand, I was barely 13 at the time. They told us they were going to speak to our parents about what Mr. Tanner had been doing to us. Over the next few days I was interviewed by a woman who asked me a lot of questions about Mr. Tanner touching my genitals. I told this person that never happened. She kept on insisting that it did and I shouldn't be afraid to say so, she said all the other boys who have been interviewed said Tanner touched them. I told her that he didn't touch me that way. She said did he ever pick you up by your pants. I said yes, so what. Did he put his hand inside your pants at the beltline? I said he could have. Then she said he could have touched your crotch area. I said I don't know. She said so it could have happened. I said I suppose so. She then said, he could have touched your genitals. I replied I guess so. After that interview, I went home totally confused. I told my mother what happened, she said that she also was interviewed by someone she didn't know. That person told her that I said Mr. Tanner used to put his hands down my pants and it* was okay to say so, that there was nothing to be ashamed of. It was Mr. Tanner who should be ashamed. "

The following week at school Mr. Tanner was gone. We all got together to talk about what was going on with Mr. Tanner. Sloan told us that if we all stuck together with the story that Mr. Tanner used to put his to hands down our pants we could make a lot of money but we all must agree. I told him why should I say that? Sloan said, because if you don't, I'll make you sorry. You don't want to fuck up everybody's chance to make money. I got scared and said okay, since everyone was looking at me as if I had the plague. So, that was the story and we all stuck to it, but I didn't like what was happening. Mr. Tanner was a cool guy and didn't deserve this. After I testified in court, I felt terrible saying those things in front of Mr. Tanner. I couldn't sleep. I was really upset. My mother saw how I was acting and asked me what's wrong? I told her everything, about agreeing to lie about Mr. Tanner, that Sloan put us up to it because we were all going to make *money. My mother called the social worker, Phyllis Marks, who came over to the house with the DA. I explained everything to them, that Sloan had pressured us to lie against Mr. Tanner so we could make a lot of money. They listened and said thank you and left."*

"A couple of weeks later after school, Sloan and Gray cornered me in the playground area and beat me up. They punched and kicked me, saying that I was fucking up their chances of making money and I better keep my mouth shut or they would shut it for me, so I said nothing. I learned later that Sloan was no longer in the case and had left school but Gray was still around, so I just went along with the program. I testified at Mr. Tanner's trial. I'm sick to my stomach and I want to make it right. Mr. Tanner does not belong in jail. I do! For doing this to him. So, whatever you need, I'll do it."

Devin was exhausted after listening to Tony. His mother was crying, saying, "Mi Tony es un buen hijo!

Como puedo ayudar?" *(Tony's a good son! What can I do to help?)*

Wayne turned off the recorder and listened to some of the playback to make sure he had it all. Devin thanked Tony and Rosa for their honesty and told them he'd be in touch with them soon. He left with Wayne, explaining that he needed to interview some of the other boys to confirm Tony's story. Wayne said he was already on it.

"Could you make me a copy of the recording?"

"I'll have it personally delivered to your office on Monday."

Devin thanked him for the good work. Walking slowly to his car, mulling it all over, he knew that if what Tony said is true, heads would roll. *Serious heads would roll.* When he got back to the hotel, he played 18 holes to wind down and relax. And his wife did, in fact, beat his ass by 10 strokes.

10

The sun was not breaking through the clouds this Monday morning, it was dark and gloomy. Devin arrived early at the office, everyone was busy preparing for what was potentially going to be a major shift in plans on the Tanner case.

About 9 o'clock a messenger showed up at Devin's office with the recording of Tony Villa and his mother. Devin rounded up Ted and Ray and listened to the recording in its entirety. When it was finished, they all sat around for a couple of minutes, digesting what they'd heard, trying to figure out where to start.

Finally, Ted began, "We need to amend Tanner's petition right away to include this newly discovered evidence. We must allege that the prosecution deliberately excluded exculpatory evidence from the defendant, which could have exonerated him due to violation of the Brady act. Are we all in agreement?"

Devin buzzed Michelle, asking her to get the recording transcribed right away, and told Ray to prepare declarations for both, Rosa Villa and her son Tony, to sign, asking to have them on his desk by noon, today. *Everyone understood their marching orders and the ball was in motion.*

Returning to his office, he called Wayne and asked him to arrange for a notary and a translator for Rosa, getting their signatures on the respective declarations.

"I need that to occur like yesterday. We need to file an amended petition by Wednesday."

Wayne confirmed, "Fax me or email me the declarations and I'll handle it from this end."

Devin then got on the phone with Judge Dana Cole's clerk, introduced himself and asked if she knew the status of the Tanner writ.

"All I can tell you is that it's on the judge's desk."

"We're in the process of filing an amended petition, so I would appreciate it if you could inform his Honor and ask him if he would, please, hold off his ruling, pending the filing of our amendment?"

"I don't think I'm at liberty to ask the judge," she said, after a moment's silence.

"I know it's out of the ordinary but, I believe the judge should have the additional information," he persisted.

"Okay, I'll run it by him," she said dubiously. Devin ended the call by assuring her it would be on his desk no later than Wednesday.

Like clockwork, it all came together on Wednesday morning. The amended petition arrived with the signed attachments by the Villas and were reviewed by Ted once more.

"I think our chances just went up 100%!" Ted exclaimed. "I don't think any judge could ignore this, regardless of how unpleasant it might look to the community at large, to have a potential reversal of a conviction for an *alleged* child molester."

Devin agreed, looking out his office window, wondering - *How did it do that? How did the sun change the gloomy sky into a brilliant, warm, sunny, electric day?*

The writ was filed by 1:15 that afternoon in Judge Cole's courtroom. The DA and AG's offices were also served. Devin was starting to believe it was going to work.

That Friday the court granted the amended petition by ordering the District Attorney's Office and the California Attorney General's office to file an opposition as to why the petition *should not* be granted, giving Tanner a new trial. They had thirty days to respond. Devin called Beverly and Jerry's family with the good news, but cautioned them to not celebrate too soon. Lots could go sideways, still. Could a miracle be in the works? *Close your eyes. Hold your breath. Cross your fingers.*

11

The following Monday, Devin meet with Jackson Mo and Jimmy Tang, at the NBC Seafood Restaurant in Monterey Park. Stephen Miao, the potential new client who was under a Federal indictment for conspiracy to distribute drugs, was also there. Devin, using his polite but aggressive style, took charge of the conversation which lasted over two hours. Fully aware that Tang and Miao were evaluating him, Devin led the discussion, focusing on getting the vital information needed to go forward with the case. *He didn't miss a beat. He was pleased with his overall performance.*

The case went before Federal Judge Garcia, who had the reputation of scaring the most hardened veteran attorneys. He was old-school. Devin told Miao he was confident that when the time came, he would eat the judge up and spit him out, which made Miao laugh out loud. He confided that his present attorney seemed to be intimidated by the judge and Devin's attitude was refreshing. Because the trial was going to be in Sacramento, potentially two weeks long, Devin knew it was vital to have Tang and Mo's input and support. At last, when the questions turned to fees, he was sure he had won them over.

Devin quoted $200,000 up front, which was all-inclusive; travel, lodging, needed experts, etc. Tang and Miao stood up, excused themselves from the table and took a walk out in front of the restaurant. Returning ten minutes Later, Tang said, "Miao likes your style. He would like you to represent him. Would you agree to accept $150,000?"

Devin didn't reply for moment. *He loved the drama of a 'pregnant pause.'* Hands together, with fingertips tapping against each other, he just sat there in silence, considering the options. He knew that Tang and Mo's share would be about $20,000. He glanced at Jackson for a clue. Jackson knew exactly what was going on in Devin's mind - they had played this game over and over in the past.

"I'm sorry for the silence, but I've been calculating whether I could accept your offer, considering everything that's at stake. So, here's what I will agree to. If you cover my travel and hotel expenses, I'll accept $170,000."

"Done!" said Tang. Since Miao had already been arraigned on the indictment and had appeared before Judge Garcia, the next court hearing would be scheduled for motions and trial setting. His current attorney, Scott Wells, was in San Francisco and Devin explained he needed to notify him immediately about the transfer of the case to him. This would happen as soon as he received the retainer fees.

Arrangements were made to have Miao give the money to Jackson, who would fly to San Francisco with him this afternoon. Devin asked Jackson to pick up Miao's file and the discovery from Wells - explaining that Michelle would email a retainer agreement for Miao to sign. Some low, polite bows, a thank you and strong handshakes were exchanged, and Tang and Miao left.

Once they were out of sight, Devin asked Jackson about *his* fees, taking into consideration that he would have to take care of Tang throughout the whole process.

"Does $20,000 sound okay?"

"I assume the fees are to be paid in cash, right?" Jackson replied, of course.

"That works for me, as long as you agree you'll be my right hand all the way through the case."

"Like always."

Devin returned to the office and immediately placed a call to Wells to discuss the orderly transfer of the file and the notification of the US Attorney and the court. The next call was to US Attorney, Eric Arnold, introducing himself as Miao's new counsel. Arnold was cordial, offering to sit down with him to discuss the case.

Devin was pleasantly surprised at the easy response. "I appreciate the offer. Once I get the file and learn more about the case, I'll take you up on it."

"Are you familiar with Judge Garcia?"

"Yes, but I've never had the privilege to appear before him."

"Then you're in for a real treat. He's a hard ass!"

"Great! Thanks for the warning. Talk soon."

12

Devin was relaxed, watching his favorite TV show, *Law and Order*, when a call came in from Jackson. "Sorry to call you at home, boss, but I just wanted to report in. The client signed the retainer and paid. I took care of Jimmy and everything went smoothly. Wells gave me the case file and the Substitution of Attorney form. He asked if after you signed it and filed it with the court, could you please send him a confirmed copy? I told him I would make sure he got it. I'm flying home tonight, when do you want to meet?"

"Good work, Jackson! Now don't get robbed on the way home. Can you come by the office tomorrow afternoon with the files and, of course, Mr. Green?" Jackson chuckled, feeling proud of his accomplishments.

Tanner's case had been in a holding pattern, awaiting the government's reply brief. Soon after Jackson showed up the following afternoon with a banker's box full of files and reports, Devin signed the Substitution of Attorney form and became the attorney of record. Jackson sat at the conference table and counted out the money. The $20 bills were stapled together in packages of hundreds. After counting it all out, he handed the package across the desk, minus his cut. Devin slowly, almost absentmindedly, put the packets of money back in the box. "What do you think of our client, Miao?"

"Well, I find it all very interesting. I sat next to him on the plane. I think he's rather young to be the kingpin of this enterprise. He is married with a couple of young children. He graduated from San Francisco State and works for his uncle's construction company, remodeling old houses in the San Francisco area. He lives with his wife, their kids and her parents, in a modest three-bedroom house in the Menlo Park district. The house may be worth $300,000. He told me he has a mortgage of $200,000; they paid $230,000 and his in-laws gave him the down payment. He drives a truck for work and his wife has a

Chevy Tahoe. His lifestyle does not represent that of drug dealer."

"Hmmm. He sure came up with the retainer easily, so looks may be deceiving, to say the least. Did you discuss the case with him?"

"No, nor did I read any of the police reports. I thought it best to leave that up to you."

"Good, though by the looks of it, it's probably going to take me a couple of days to read through the file."

"Wells told me a lot of it was on CDs and DVDs, that he had all of it downloaded, that's why the file looks so fat."

"After I've read everything, I'd like to visit with the client in San Francisco, then have further discussions with Arnold, to see how he views the evidence against Miao. I expect I could be ready by the end of the week. I want you to fly up with me."

"Okay, just let me know."

"I'll have Michelle make the arrangements and give you a heads-up in advance. Thanks for the great job." Jackson nodded and left.

Devin asked Michelle to advise Judge Garcia's clerk that they were coming into the case and find out when the next court date was, and what the court expected from us for that hearing.

Michelle had become re-energized with the return of Devin and the fast-paced activity throughout the office. She couldn't help sounding a bit like a 'groupie' as she blurted out, "It's so good to have you back!" *Thanks.*

It took the whole afternoon and into early evening just to identify and index the contents of the Baker's box; from the pleadings, to the police reports, the witness statements, the search warrants and affidavits, and the pictures and videos. He took a long, deep breath... he would start his review the following morning. *Right now, he needed to go home to his wife and a glass of good wine.*

13

It had all started in the summer of 2009, when the police got a telephone call from a person identifying herself as Ann Wallace. She told the following story:

She lived in a housing development in Oakdale, just outside of Sacramento. Because of the real estate crash, a lot of the houses on her street were vacant and went up for sale. After a couple of houses on her block were sold, she was told by the realtor that families were going to be moving in. She thought that was good and it would help the neighborhood, but no one moved in. Soon she started to notice that there were some young men of Asian descent, coming and going into the sold homes, usually at night; staying for a few hours and then leaving, carrying garbage bags from the houses, loading them into a black SUV and driving off. That's when she first noticed the windows in the houses were blacked out from the inside. This activity went on for a few months. She became suspicious when the property was not being kept up and she was sure no one actually lived there. Her suspicions rose and she thought that she should report it. Her inquiry was handed over to Sgt. Bill Hoolihan of the Oakwood Police Department, by Detective Dan McFarland. He was asked to check out the properties located on Walnut Street. A few days later, he drove by and stopped at one of the residences. It looked unoccupied, so he decided to walk the property. He first knocked on the door, checking for occupants. No answer. He tried to peer into the blacked-out windows but couldn't see inside at all. Walking around the side and back of the house, he noticed those windows were also blacked-out. The rear yard was full of weeds and in total disrepair. Among the weeds, he found some electrical wiring running from the house into the garage. He returned to his police cruiser and called McFarland, explaining what he saw. McFarland asked him to stick around, he was going to make a couple of calls.

He called Northern California Water and Power and spoke with a Bob Casias, who advised him that the electric and water bills for that address were triple the regular bills for an average home in that area. McFarland asked for a customer name at that home and the response was, Philip Ching Construction Company, in Oakland. McFarland asked how long the outsized billing had been going on. The answer was, six months.

McFarland called Hoolihan back and updated him on the findings with the utility company. Acknowledging something was not kosher with the house, McFarland checked with the county recorder's office and discovered the name of the owner was the same construction company paying the utility bills. The deed was recorded approximately six months earlier.

Hoolihan then contacted Mrs. Wallace, the concerned neighbor who had called. She was excited to see him. She told him that the property had been on the market for sale by Julie Chen, an agent of Allied Realty, and that she had spoken with her when she put up the SOLD sign. Chen had told her a nice family was going to be her neighbor. However, she'd never seen anyone move in, just a few trucks that originally arrived and parked backwards, inside the garage. She didn't see what they were doing, but they came and went a few times, staying for a few hours each time. That's when she noticed that the windows had all been blacked out. Concerned about what this all meant, she had decided to report it to the police.

Hoolihan thanked her and told her to keep her eyes and ears open as he gave her his business card. He returned to the station house and discussed the next move with McFarland. They both agreed they needed to speak with Julie Chen, the realtor.

McFarland made the telephone call to Julie Chen, explaining he was investigating activity surrounding a property that she recently sold. She was very cooperative, explaining that Allied was selling bank-owned repo's in the Oakdale area. They had over a hundred listings and she had personally sold about twenty houses to four different companies from the Oakland and San Francisco area, within the Last eight to nine months. The banks had qualified them and they got in with no down payment, but paid the banks' asking price. She had been told they were going to remodel the properties and then put them on the rental market until the housing market rebounded. Julie explained that this was common practice these days; companies with cash were getting properties at rock-bottom prices. The goal was to make a fortune in the future; meantime, the rental income would cover part of the overhead. It was a win-win for them and the bank.

He asked who she had dealt with on the Walnut Street property. She replied Phillip Cheng and his assistant, Sarah Wu. He asked if she could provide the addresses for the other 18 properties. She needed clearance from her boss. McFarland explained that the houses were probably being used for illegal purposes and wanted to check out the other properties, just in case. She got her boss, Alan Dean, on the phone and McFarland laid out the issues and his needs. An hour later, he received an email with the list of all 18 properties.

It took three days for them to canvas each house. They all had blacked out windows, exactly like the houses on Walnut. Additional checks with the utility company came up with the same results. The Sacramento Sheriff's Department had been called in for assistance because the Oakdale Police Department only had eight officers and this was way too big for them to handle. The Sheriff's Department brought in the DEA as part of the investigation team. Surveillance on the properties was set up as part of the investigation, and owners of the companies who acquired the subject properties, were also placed under surveillance.

Almost immediately, it became obvious that the companies were related to one another. The DEA secured wiretaps on the principles, all were of Asian descent; however, *Miao's name never came up in any of the wire taps.* The police observed some young Asian men showing up at the houses, all the houses, usually at night, staying between five and six hours, then leaving, and returning a couple of days later. After about a month, the activity changed by way of a black SUV Range Rover showing up at each house, entering through the garage, its four occupants getting out and entering the house through the front door. Later, they were seen exiting with dark green garbage bags that were loaded into the vehicle, then quickly driving off. They were surveilled all the way to a warehouse on Pier 39 in San Francisco, where they unloaded the vehicle. This exercise was repeated over the next few days at all the other houses. The surveillance teams recorded all this activity on video.

Over the next few days, David Loftin, the DEA agent in charge, reviewed all the surveillance tapes. His opinion, with the concurrence of McFarland, who continued to be part of the task force, as well as, other involved law enforcement officers, was that the houses were being used to grow marijuana. It fit all the criteria. Loftin contacted US Attorney, Lawrence Markey, to secure search warrants for the warehouse in San Francisco, the corporate offices of the companies involved, the residences of the principles and all the locations where they believed the marijuana was being grown. It had to be a surprise move. The searches all needed to be simultaneous, this was going to require a great deal of manpower.

Since the DEA was now heading up the investigation and multiple counties were involved, the case was turned over to the US Attorney's Office in Sacramento. Incredibly, the searches all went off without a hitch. Almost a ton of marijuana was discovered in the warehouse in San Francisco, along with over $400,000 in cash. Six individuals were arrested at that location, all identified by previous surveillance footage, showing them coming and going to the grow houses. In each house, grow trays containing marijuana plants in early stages of growth, grow lights, drying tables and items used to grow the plants, were found. In Loftin's opinion, each house could produce at least 200 to 300 pounds in three cycles per year. That equated to somewhere between 600 and 900 pounds a year. If multiplied by 20 houses, priced at approximately $500 a pound, he figured the enterprises were earning around $400-$500 million a year. It was his biggest bust ever!

All the searches were video recorded with forensics lifting over 100 fingerprints, hoping to match them up to potential suspects. The business records from the various companies revealed additional houses in Fresno and Modesto. Ten additional Asian males were arrested, bringing the total to sixteen. Loftin supervised the collection of all the evidence - it was a monumental task. The original indictment included the names of all sixteen arrestees, but Miao's identity did not surface until a couple of the minor players, who were offered plea deals for their cooperation, pointed the finger at Stephen Miao, as the ringleader. He was named as the one who ran the entire operation; from the purchase of the houses, to installation of the equipment, and the supervision of the growing and distribution of the marijuana. They claimed he had a partner named Felix Wong, who had fled to Hong Kong when the busts went down. Supposedly, Miao and Wong had been friends since high school; they both worked for Felix's father who owned three Chinese restaurants in Chinatown. The father, also believed to be the head of a Chinese gang from Taiwan, took them under his wing, taught them the business, and when he died, they continued their criminal activities in San Francisco's Chinatown. It's believed that during this time, the idea of the present enterprise came to fruition

    The police only had *hearsay* information about Miao's involvement in all this. They needed a lot more if they were going to charge him. They checked to see if he had any criminal record. He had none. They checked his DMV records and obtained his picture and fingerprints. They compared his prints with several unknown prints that had been obtained from various locations and came up with two hits. One was from the garage area of a residence, and one from an electrical box in another. They showed his picture to Julie Chen, she recognized his picture. She said he was the person who came with this Ms. Wu on a few occasions, during the purchase process. She did not actually speak to him, but she saw him going through a few of the houses, pending the sale. He was identified as the contractor who was going to do the remodeling work on the houses. *Loftin cringed because that could easily explain why his prints were in a couple of the houses.* While checking Miao's background, they had found that he had graduated from San Francisco State with a degree in electrical engineering, at this point, they were still operating only on the words of the cooperating witnesses.

Part of the task force was involved in tracking where the equipment was purchased to grow the weed. They had the names of the manufactures who, in turn, gave them a list of retailers in the northern California area. McFarland's group followed the manufacturer's trail to a small hardware store in

Marin County which had ordered over $250,000 worth of growing equipment which set off alarm bells. They checked out the store and found it closed and stripped to the walls. The landlord of the shopping center said they disappeared into the night. The owner was Sam Woo. They were informed by his wife that he was in Hong Kong. She told the investigators that she worked in the store from time to time and did the books. They showed her a picture of Miao she thought she recognized him, that he did business with her husband. That's all she knew. They asked her why the store had suddenly closed... and why did her husband go to Hong Kong? She explained that one night, about a month ago, he got a telephone call and immediately after that he told her he had to leave for China, that he would explain later. She said she was shocked but said nothing. They asked her what happened to the inventory of the store and she again said she didn't know; that her husband said he had sold everything and would send her the money that he received from its sale. She had no idea when he was returning.

At this point, Loftin thought he might have enough to pick up Miao and see if he would talk. They went to his residence and noticed a black Range Rover in the driveway. A quick check showed it was registered to Miao's father-in-law who also happened to be residing at the residence. The vehicle description matched the SUV that frequently visited the grow houses, but the license plate number was different. Miao was polite and cooperative, claiming to know nothing about the marijuana business. He explained that as a favor to his high school friend, he had visited some properties in the Sacramento area that he might possibly be interested in buying to remodel and sell. His friend had asked him to accompany him and give him some ideas about the remodeling potential, which he did, however it had never materialized into any work.

Loftin asked, "What about the purchasing of items from a hardware store in Marin?"

"Oh, yeah. That's true. The owner was a friend of my uncles, so we gave him some business whenever we needed supplies for our construction business."

Although it all sounded legit to him, it just seemed too convenient, too perfect, so Loftin told him that two of the defendants had agreed to cooperate and they had fingered him as the ringleader. "Did you know Solomon Chin and Frank La?"

He seemed to catch his breath at the suddenness of the question. He hesitated and then said, "Yes, I think so. They used to work for Felix but I can't understand why they would accuse me!" Loftin thanked Miao for answering his questions and left the residence, thinking he needed more time, he just wasn't buying it.

The following morning Loftin received a telephone call from Detective Jim Fisher. He advised him that he had traced the records of the manufacturer of the grow Lamps purchased through the Marin hardware store. They had been shipped directly to the warehouse on Pier 39, he'd looked at the signed receipts.

"Well, who signed for them?"

"I can't tell, but it looks like Felix Wong." Loftin asked for the receipt copies and immediately contacted Eric Arnold at the US Attorney's office, bringing him up to speed. He asked him to secure a search warrant for Miao's residence and the bLack SUV parked there.

"I don't know," Arnold said. "I'll see if I can get the duty judge to sign off, your probable cause is weak."

"Bullshit! We have two accomplices giving him up, and he had connections to the Marin County hardware store where over $250,000 worth of 'grow Lamps' were purchased and shipped directly to the warehouse on Pier 39 in San Francisco. Plus, there's a black SUV Range Rover in the driveway of his house which matches the description of the one seen at the crime scenes. What's weak about that? What more do you need?"

"Okay. You've made your point!"

Loftin called McFarland and asked him to check the evidence file for the surveillance pictures of the black Range Rover, wanting to compare them to the pictures taken of the vehicle in Miao's driveway.

Later that afternoon, while comparing pictures of the license plates, they noted that they were completely different. When they had run the SUV plates at the crime scene, they'd received a 'no such number' report but it was now obvious that the letter and numbers had been altered with tape to make them look different.

"Bingo! It's the same vehicle! This was too big a coincidence." He called Arnold and asked for his search warrant.

"I was just about to call you. I have it here, signed off by Judge John Card, himself. I'll fax it over to you right now."

"Is it okay for a nighttime search?" Arnold replied no.

Loftin looked at his watch, it was 3:10 PM. He moved quickly, assembling a search team to accompany him and they arrived at Miao's house at 4:30 sharp!

Miao's wife answered the door, explaining that Miao was not home nor was the black SUV. "My father has it and he's out for the day... I don't know when he'll return."

Loftin showed her the warrant as six officers entered the house, searching and videotaping their activities for over two hours. They seized computers, a couple of filing cabinets full of files and bank records. There was no evidence of contraband anywhere.

Finally, they were done and Miao's wife signed off on a seized property list. Loftin thanked her for her cooperation, left his business card and asked her to have her husband call him. Walking away, he was upset because the SUV was not there and he'd had his forensic team ready to go over it with a fine- tooth comb. *Dammit! He wondered if he would ever see it again.*

The following day Miao showed up at the DEA's headquarters asking for Loftin. He was livid, ranting, "If you wanted to search, all you had to do was ask! You have seriously upset my family. If you want to arrest me, go ahead - but leave my family alone!"

Loftin responded calmly, "Sorry, it's just business. By the way, I *would* like to examine your Range Rover."

Miao replied, "First, it's not mine. I don't even have keys for it. You need to ask my father-in-law, it's his car."

"How do I get in touch with him?"

"I don't know. All I know is, he's away on business. I'm not his caretaker."

Loftin relished the moment. He moved closer and replied, "I guess I'll take you up on your offer. You are under arrest for conspiracy to distribute marijuana." He turned him around and handcuffed him. He called in US Marshal Billy Gevov to book him, telling Miao to call his Lawyer as he was being escorted out of the office, his face drained of color and his jaw clenched tightly.

Loftin called Arnold and said, "Listen, I might've jumped the gun with Miao. He came into my office with an attitude so I arrested him. I need you to get me an indictment right now. I'm available to come to the courthouse with a couple of my detectives, and I think we can produce enough evidence to get an indictment."

"Damn, you're difficult," Arnold responded. "I'm supposed to be in court tomorrow morning taking guilty pleas on the last of the group."

"I want you to include Felix Wong in your presentation. He's Miao's partner. I have him signing the receipt for the grow lamp equipment."

"Great! Now I'll have to work all night."

"Hey, being a lawman is a tough job, right?" He had put out a warrant on the Range Rover but nothing had turned up.

The next day, Arnold secured the indictment and Miao appeared in the Magistrate's Court accompanied by his attorney, Scott Wells, pled 'not guilty' and was released on bond.

Devin was exhausted from his review of the reports of the various officers, their logs, the surveillance and search videos. But he knew that, even with all this, something was missing. What they had was a couple of Miao's prints in a couple of houses; evidence that he'd been doing business with Marin hardware; a black SUV in his driveway. All this was explained. What was still troubling Devin was that the two Felix Wong gangsters had turned on Miao pointing the finger at him. But where's the money? Where's the lifestyle?

That's what's *still* missing. He suddenly remembered the famous line from the movie Jerry Mc Quire, "*Show Me the* Money." That's it! He called Ted, giving him the basics of the case and all the unconnected dots...

"That's genius! Show me the money works! The cops will embellish the amount of the drugs and the huge profits the bad guys make, as they usually do, to make it as big as their egos. It's going to play directly into our hands."

Devin was thinking he needed to speak with Miao... meet his family... quickly get a feel for his lifestyle. Brilliant!

14

Michelle called out to Devin saying Wright was on the line. Devin picked up the phone. "I've located three of the boys, including Sloan, who is now living in Memphis Tennessee where he has a pending robbery case," he almost shouted. "I spoke with his father and asked if we could speak to his son about the Tanner case. He asked me why, so I told him that we're trying to get him a new trial. The father sounded really pissed off and asked why his son should help you? I told him that we have statements from the other boys saying that they had lied against Tanner to get money, and that his son was also included." Wright caught his breath for a second and continued. "The old man said that his son was in serious trouble and that if you could help him out he would help you out. I didn't know how to respond to that, so I told him I'd get back to him. As for the other two boys, Ray Ruiz and Michael Sanchez, they are now living in Bakersfield and are roommates attending Bakersfield Junior college. I talked to them too, and they said they would cooperate, but only if they didn't have to give back the money. I told them that I didn't think that would be a problem. I have tentatively set up a meeting with them a week from Tuesday and I think you need to be there."

Devin replied, I'll try to be there but if I can't, I'll have Ray Flores or Ted Cohen of my office attend."

"What about Sloan?"

"We can't bargain for his story. However, we could hire the best criminal defense lawyer in Tennessee who might be able to make a sweetheart deal, what do you think?"

Wayne replied, "From my point of view, his father is white trash. Probably has already spent all the money or is not willing to spend it for his son's defense. It's my understanding the boy has a public defender and is in custody"

"Do you know how much his bail is?

"I believe its $100,000."

"Call back Sloan's father and tell him that if his son gives us a truthful declaration, we'll hire the best defense attorney for his son and get him released on bond, at no expense to him."

The next day, Wayne called Devin back and shouted, "Guess what? It worked! I have the PD's name and the case number for you."

Devin said, "Great work! But before we take any action on that, we need to get his story and a signed declaration. See if you can make those arrangements right away. Ted knows a retired, Tennessee Supreme Court Judge, whose son is a top-notch criminal defense lawyer with lots of political clout. I'll set the wheels in motion, but I want Sloan's interview conducted under oath and taken before a court reporter."

Devin call Beverly and explained the situation with Sloan, explaining that all legal fees and bail money would have to come from an independent source because if it was connected to Tanner, it would destroy his credibility and would be worthless. It would also taint the other kids' statements. All I can do is to refer you to Attorney Ellis. All arrangements must be made between the parties, absent any connection to Tanner. I cannot be a party to it."

Beverly asked, "What should I do?"

Devin replied, "You'll just have to figure that out on your own. Get my drift?"

She replied, "Okay, give me the attorney's name again." Devin said, *this conversation never happened.*

Two days later Devin received the opposition brief, which of course, contradicted everything in Tanner's Petition; basically, calling Tony Villa and his mother liars, and further disputed the legal reasoning for Tanner's failure to testify. Devin knew that they weren't going to take this lying down – it was going to be a fight to the finish. Judge Cole set a status conference to be heard in five days. He indicated that he was going to set a schedule for a full-blown evidentiary hearing, covering all issues raised in the pleadings.

Devin sat down with Ted to plan their strategy going forward. They both would attend the status conference. Since it was obviously a contested hearing, they would need to have Tanner present. Ted prepared and filed an ex- parte motion to have Tanner moved from state prison to the Vista Court County lockup for the duration of the hearings. The judge signed the order and Tanner was transferred within two days to the San Diego County Sheriff's lockup in Vista.

Tanner knew Ted, but this was the first-time Devin laid eyes on him. Just prior to the proceedings, the three of them had a brief meeting. Devin explained as much as he could about the process about to take place, trying to assure him, asking him to take a deep breath as this was going to be a long ride.

The judge called everyone into chambers, excluding Tanner. Everybody introduced themselves, trying to keep it very casual. The prosecution was being handled by Assistant Attorney General Michael Rawlings, since the DA's who were involved in the prior trial would necessarily be witnesses. The discussion was brief. The judge wanted to know how much time was needed to prepare for the hearing.

Devin responded, "Four to six months, as there are still witnesses that need to be interviewed. Plus, we plan to call a couple of experts, not yet chosen. We also expect to have several pretrial motions that the court will need to consider."

Rawlings explained to the judge that he had just come aboard and didn't believe he could be ready before six months, either. The judge considered everyone's input and said. "Let's go out and put all this on the record, setting the hearing date out six months. However, I'm setting another status conference within thirty days. At that time, I want reports on your progress and I expect cooperation from both sides. The burden is on you, Mr. O'Neill," he concluded.

"I understand, Your Honor. I know we are going to get a fair hearing."

"Yes. Both sides will get a fair hearing."

Ted had a good feeling there would be no hometown decision here. After lunch, they visited with Tanner for a couple of hours in lockup. Ted explained that they wanted him to take a polygraph exam and be examined by a psychiatrist specializing in child molestation cases. Ted said, "I expect your full cooperation." Tanner assured them he'd comply.

Since the status conference had conflicted with Wayne Wright's interview with the boys in Bakersfield, Ray went to the interview, giving him questions from time to time, but otherwise stayed in the background. The reason for that was, in case the boys changed their story in court,

Wright could testify as to what they said in the interview. *Hopefully that was not going to happen*. The next day, Ray gave Devin an overview of the interviews. He had a copy of the audio recordings which Michelle had transcribed, confirming that money had been paid to seal their lips. However, since the others involved were *outing* them, they wanted to get on the same bandwagon. They did not want "bad karma" following them, they'd said. They were willing to testify.

Devin listened intently to the whole update, telling Ray the start date for the hearing that subpoenas needed to be served on the boys... *we don't want them disappearing on us.*

15

Devin flew to San Francisco with Mo to meet with Miao. When they arrived at Miao's residence Devin noted that it was in a middle-class neighborhood, nothing to brag about. He met Miao's wife and their two children, both girls, ages six and eight, and the mother-in-law. As they sat around the dining room table Devin was pleased to see that the surroundings were very average. A far cry from a drug dealer's lifestyle, especially someone who the DEA believed was making millions of dollars. Miao answered Devin's questions about his background, his education and his work history. Then Devin asked him about Felix Wong.

He said that they had been friends since they were six years old. Miao's father worked for Felix's father in his restaurant business in Chinatown. He was 14 when his father died and that's when Felix's father kind of took over the role as a surrogate parent. He helped with the family finances and gave him a job working at one of his restaurants. Felix and he were tight, close friends.

Devin then asked if Felix's father was a gangster.

"That's what the word on the street was, but I don't personally know. All I know is that he was very good to me and to my family. When he died, it was a big blow to me and Felix. We were both attending University at the time. Felix dropped out of school but I continued, wanting to earn my degree. That's when my relationship with him kind of faltered, we cared for each other but we did not really run in the same circles anymore."

Devin asked "Do you know anything about his business side?"

"He took over his father's business enterprises, including the restaurants."

"Did you ever do any business with him?"

"Not really. I remodeled his home in Sausalito and he referred me to some of his friends and business associates when they needed my services".

"Are you aware you were identified, along with other persons, as a group who purchased houses outside of Sacramento which were used to grow marijuana? In fact, your fingerprints were found in two of those houses."

"Yes, the police told me. I explained to them that I had been to a few of the homes because some of Felix's friends wanted my advice about possibly doing remodeling work in that area but unfortunately no business ever materialized from that.

"Have you ever been to a warehouse on Pier 39 in San Francisco?" *Miao replied no.* "What about Sam Woo, you know him?"

"Yes, of course. He was a good friend of my uncle. When we needed supplies, we would order them from him?"

"I need to know why Chin and La would identify you as the ringleader of the marijuana business?"

Miao shook his head, "I'd like to know that myself! I know them both from my years of working at Felix's dad's restaurant. They were always very close and protective of Felix. Maybe they want to divert attention away from Felix and lay the blame on me. I don't know, I swear I'm not involved.

"Do you know where Felix is?" *Yes, he's in China.*

"Are you in contact with him?" *I'd rather not say.*

"If you're not involved and live the lifestyle that I've observed, where did you get the cash to pay my fees?" *Felix. That's all I can say.*

Devin shifted his body, sitting directly in front of Miao, looking him directly in the eye. "I want you to know you have my complete confidence, okay? So, I want to ask you about the Range Rover. It seems the police are very interested in it."

Miao replied, "It's my father-in-law's. He has allowed various people to use the vehicle from time to time."

"Do you have anything to do with lending out the vehicle?" *It's not for me to say.*

"Do you know where the vehicle is now?" *It's gone.*

"If the police question your father-in-law about the vehicle, what's he going to say?" *Not much. He is on vacation in China until this all blows over.*

"Okay. I want to take some video of you, your home, your family and your business, to show your simple lifestyle. I would also like a list of people who have known you, professionals; like your accountant, your banker, clergy and other pillars of the community who would be willing to testify as to your character. When I leave here today, I'm going to talk with the US attorney handling your case and see what they want, I'll give you a call to discuss the outcome of that meeting. Jackson will handle the videotaping, if's that's okay?" *Of course.*

Devin took the short flight to Sacramento. He arrived at the Federal Courthouse on A Street, standing there in all its glory. An architect's dream, very modern, with tons of marble and granite – taxpayers' money well spent. The US Attorney's Office was on the sixth floor, also very posh. After being announced, Eric Arnold greeted him. Eric was a short man in his early 40's, with piercing blue eyes and an infectious smile. Devin, always quick on the analysis, thought, he probably does well with the ladies and juries, if he can speak.

They sat down in the conference room. David Loftin, the DEA agent joined them. Eric asked Devin if it was okay? What could Devin say but "sure." Devin did nearly all the listening. Eric advised him that all 16 of the defendants had pled guilty but only two were willing to testify against Miao.

Loftin butted in and said, "Really, I don't believe your client is the main man, but he's up there. We need details about who their customers are, where's the money flow… we want to bring down their house. If your client will cooperate, he will only face five years. We're pretty confident this is an international crime syndication headed by Felix Wong."

Devin held his breath for a few seconds before finally responding, "Just because my client and Wong have been lifelong friends doesn't mean he knows about or is involved in Wong's business dealings."

"Crap! Sure, he is!"

Eric raised his voice to Loftin, "Let's be civil! Devin is way above your pay grade."

Devin smiled to himself, thinking, these guys are playing good guy - bad guy. Pretty obvious, and amateurish. He said, "I'll discuss your offer with my client. I'm not necessarily interested in pitching it, because, frankly, after my review of all the evidence, including your informants', I think I can win this."

"Good luck with that," Loftin smirked. *Devin thought, cop mentality.* Devin thanked Eric for the meeting, saying he'd get back to him.

Eric responded as he got up to leave, "The pretrial is coming up. Garcia will want to know where we all stand."

"I know. Thank you." Devin was exhausted, decided to stay the night and flew back to LA the following morning.

16

Ray picked him up at LAX and asked to be filled in about the meeting, as they drove back to the office. Devin put his sunglasses on and relaxed into the passenger seat, gathering his thoughts.

"Things went reasonably well. However, I think our client is lying through his teeth. He completely denies any involvement but his answers to my questions speak volumes. And considering the evidence that the prosecution *thinks* it has, the door to our '*show me the money*' defense is wide open. I think Miao can pull it off, but the serious fly in the ointment is the finger-pointing by the two informers. I need to find out why they turned on Miao. They worked for Felix for a long time, and somehow, I don't think he would approve of their actions. If I could find some motive for their actions, I could impeach their credibility. I need a whole lot more than '*they just lied to save their own asses and that's* why *they agreed to a plea deal.*"

Back at the office Devin called Jackson, explaining that he needed someone in the Chinese community who could dig up something in their backgrounds. Chin and La's disdain for Miao needed to be explained. It didn't make sense that they would just rat him out. If it was theirs, he was sure they would've just taken their medicine. Besides, he was sure that Wong would cover for them if necessary.

Jackson replied, "That's not going to be easy, Devin. They are part of a Chinese criminal syndicate, headed by Felix." He breathed heavily and continued, "I'll have a private talk with Miao. I'll take care of it, boss."

"Thanks. I know you will."

As soon as Devin hung up the phone, he twirled his chair around and started to refocus on the Tanner matter. Wright had arranged for an interview with Sloan at the Memphis County jail, however, his public defender had insisted on being present. Wayne informed Devin that he had a court reporter standing by all that was needed was his timetable. Devin responded that next Thursday Wayne replied,

"Fine. I'll be there a day earlier to make sure there are no hitches in our plans."

Devin's flight to Memphis went through Dallas and, as usual, there was a schedule delay. Devin sat in the first-class lounge for what seemed like an eternity. He always hated taking this flight to Memphis with its par-for-the-course delays. Finally, he arrived in Memphis at 11:00, Wayne picked him up. The interview was scheduled for 10 the following morning. Once at the hotel, Devin went straight to bed, exhausted from the day's travel. He wanted to be sharp and ready for tomorrow. *Sloan could be Tanner's savior if he was sincere.*

The ride from the hotel to the jail took about twenty minutes. The building was old, Southern architecture, as Devin remembered from movies he'd seen. It stood three stories high with stately white pillars in the front. Wayne had done a good job arranging everything. He introduced

Dick Blount, Sloan's public defender, to Devin on the front steps. They chatted for a few minutes before going in.

"Let me handle the jailers," Blount said. "I know them all. They're good Ol' Southern boys."

When they entered through the front doors, they walked down a long hallway, hearing their loud footsteps on the old, shiny wooden floors. At the end, was a small desk with a police sergeant seated in front of what looked like a steel door. He stood up and shook Blount's hand. Blount introduced Devin and Wayne and he shook their hands, saying with a toothy grin, 'any friend of Dick's is a friend of mine.' Then he explained, "We have set up an interview room for you on this floor. Your court reporter is already there waiting for you."

"Thank you, Sergeant."

A large key was produced by the Sergeant who opened the steel door where an officer was waiting to escort them to the interview room. He pointed to the door saying 'that's the room – let me know when you want the inmate brought in.'

"Thank you. Now's a good time."

Ten minutes later Sloan was brought in. He looked like a character from an old chain-gang movie, complete with a black and white striped jail uniform. He was surprisingly tall, over six foot two, very thin, short blonde hair, wearing a very weak goatee. He was handcuffed at the waist.

Introductions were made all around. The officer put Sloan in a chair, handcuffing him to it, as he left the room, saying he'd be right outside. Blount talked first, explaining to Sloan why he was there. Once he'd been briefed and agreed to cooperate with the process, Devin took over. The court reporter administered the oath. *Devin prayed that he would tell the truth.* After about an hour and a half, Devin had no more questions, he was happy with the responses he got.

Sloan seemed candid and explained his role in the farce that had convicted Tanner. For him it was about the money. The opportunity just presented itself. The police wanted to believe that Tanner was a child molester, so it was easy; the school paid off big time. He didn't know how much, since his father handled all that. All he had to do was keep the others in line. A short time after he had testified at the preliminary hearing, he had a conversation with the DA who told him that Tony Villa was backtracking. She had asked him to talk to him so he did. Later, the DA told him they didn't need him anymore since he had done such a good job.

Devin asked, "Did you beat up Tony?"

"Yeah, I regret that now. Tell him I'm sorry."

When they were off the record, Devin thanked him for his honesty and explained that he should be out of jail within the next couple of days. Blount went to find the jailer who came into the room and took Sloan away. Devin had a flash of pity for the kid. *What a poor soul, he thought, but was glad he'd gotten what he came for and more.* He asked Wayne to wait for the transcript of the interview and ask Sloan to review it and sign it.

Afterwards, Devin had a conversation with Beverly, explaining how the Sloan interview had gone. He confirmed the green light to proceed with the plans to get him out of this mess. Devin slept all the way home on the flight to LAX that evening.

17

He only had two days before he had to appear at Miao's pretrial before Judge Garcia. He sat down with Ted to create a strategy. He already knew he needed to keep quiet about the *"show me the money"* defense strategy until his closing argument.

Ted started, "You need to give the prosecution enough rope to hang themselves. Let them run with the position that this was one of the largest drug busts in their history, try and keep them off guard. Always keep them wondering where you're going. I just hope you can neutralize the two turncoats. What do you think?"

"Oh, I'm sure the judge will want to know what our defense is."

"So, start off by telling him that he is innocent and that all the prosecution's evidence can easily be explained away. Man, I'd like to be there to watch the show."

"I have to give them a witness list and an exhibit list," Devin continued. "I don't think the witnesses will be any trouble but the exhibits could alert them; like the videos of the house, the family and his business, his tax returns, bank statements - all needed to show a standard of living. If they were for impeachment only I wouldn't need to disclose, but I can't take the chance that if I don't disclose them in the beginning, the judge might exclude them. That would be disastrous."

Ted said, "So go ahead and disclose. You've got to take that chance. Just go for it."

The hearing was scheduled for 2:30 that afternoon. Devin flew to Sacramento that morning and met Miao for lunch, where he explained the purpose of the hearing. When Devin arrived on the ninth floor, he approached the front of courtroom C. The doors were open so he walked into the empty courtroom. He approached the clerk who was seated to the left of the bench and introduced himself.

She looked at her watch and said in a hushed voice, "Mr. O'Neill, you're early." Devin remarked that he was just getting the lay of the land.

She smiled and said, "I'm Laurel. I've been Judge Garcia's clerk for nearly twenty years and now, I pretty much run the show." She handed Devin a business card and said, "If there's anything you need, just call me. I have the judge's ear."

Devin thanked her as he left the courtroom, "I'll wait outside for my client. Fifteen minutes later, Miao arrived with an entourage of four people. Devin told them to wait outside and keep their distance when the hearing got started because the cops would be checking them out if they knew they were with Miao. Within minutes, Arnold and Loftin got off the elevator. Devin greeted them and led them into the courtroom, asking Miao to wait outside. Once inside, Arnold and Loftin took their seats at counsel table. The bailiff (US Marshal) was now in the courtroom and the court reporter was seated in front of the witness stand. *Everything was in order, finally!*

Laurel motioned to Devin, "Mr. O'Neill, would you have your client sit down next to you at counsel table?" Devin replied, of course. A few minutes, later the judge appeared, everyone rose from their seats. Before the bailiff could even speak, the judge was up on the bench. He was a slight man with short gray hair. Devin could see that he was wearing a white T-shirt and jeans under his robe. *Devin liked that.* Once on the bench, you immediately knew he was in charge. He looked over the courtroom in a slow, deliberate manner. Besides the court staff, Devin, Miao, Arnold and Loftin were the only ones there.

Laurel called the case USA versus Miao. The judge asked everyone to please sit down and identify themselves, for the record. Each side took their turn at the podium, located between counsel tables. When Devin stood up and identified himself, the judge said, "Mr.

O'Neill, I don't recognize you, is this the first time you've been in my Court?"

Devin was surprised at the direct comments by the judge. "Yes, Your Honor. And I'm sure it will be a pleasurable experience."

The judge laughed and said, "I guess you haven't heard about me."

"To the contrary, Your Honor. That's why I *know* I'm going to enjoy this experience." *He glanced casually at Arnold and could tell he was getting upset at the thought of being ignored in this exchange of familiarity.*

The judge opened the paperwork that was before him and remarked, "We'll see. We'll see." They got promptly down to business and in less than twenty minutes, they were out of the courtroom with a trial date set for forty days out. The court stated that all motions must be filed at least fifteen days before the trial, with witness and exhibit lists to be exchanged at that time. The judge explained his courtroom hours were Monday thru Friday, from 8:30 to 4 p.m. *Devin could tell that Arnold was intimidated by the judge by his demeanor. Not he... the tougher the judge, usually the fairer the* trial. *He had come to understand that through the years.*

When they left the courthouse, Miao said that he'd had a meeting with Jackson about the witnesses, and that he had done some checking on his own. He explained that he'd given all his information to Jackson and directed him to certain people he should talk to.

"That's our biggest hurdle, at this point," commented Devin.

Miao shook his head and responded, "I think you'll find out that it's not going to be a problem." He then offered to drive Devin back to the airport since he had driven from San Francisco for the court hearing. Devin accepted. His flight landed just in time to catch rush-hour.

Three days later, Jackson called Devin and said, "I have great news. I think your worries are over. I have enough info to bury your adversaries! When do you want to meet?"

"Today's not soon enough - we have a trial date in five weeks."

18

Devin met with Ted for an update on the progress of the Tanner case. Ted explained he had obtained a court order for Tanner to be examined by Dr. Sam Miles, head of the psychiatric panel for the Los Angeles Superior Court, with an expertise in pedophilia.

"The examination is scheduled for tomorrow at the jail facilities in Vista. Ray is going to attend the session, hopefully it will be fruitful. Also, Michael Rawlings, whom I found out is a good friend of Brent Romney, I think maybe it's a good idea to bring Brent on board, but I'll leave that decision up to you. I've also been in contact with Mike Williams, he was the polygraph examiner on the OJ case years back. He's willing to go to San Diego, however, I'm concerned that if I get a court order, the prosecution is going to be aware of it. Then if he doesn't pass the polygraph, they'll connect the dots if we don't present anything about it during trial."

Devin thought about it and said, "Forget it. Since the results are not admissible anyway, why create a negative. Let's just pass on the polygraph."

Ted continued, "We also need an expert to testify on the issue of 'ineffectiveness of trial counsel'. Do you have any thoughts about that?"

Devin replied, "Yes, we need someone that the judge knows about and respects."

"I agree. Preferably somebody from the San Diego area. I'll investigate and come up with some names."

"I'll do the same. The hearing will be on us before we know it, so any expert we hire is going to have to review the entire trial transcript, plus everything else we have, so their opinion will be valuable and credible. Let's move quickly and give it our priority."

"I'm on it," agreed Ted, as he grabbed his notebook and folder full of notes, making a dash for the door.

"I'll give Romney a call to see if he has an interest in coming on board," Devin shouted out to him as he bolted down the hall to the elevator.

He returned to his desk and grabbed the phone, buzzing for Michelle. His mind was still focused on Miao, but he knew he needed to make sure the Tanner case was also moving forward. Once Michelle got Romney on the phone, Devin explained the Tanner case.

Brent was excited at the prospect of joining forces with Devin. "Of course, you can count on me! I love working with you and from what you tell me about the case, it's a serious miscarriage of justice."

"Great! I'll advise the court that you're joining the defense team. I will cover your fees. How do you want to work it?"

"I think an hourly fee would be fair to the client. Shall we call it at $300 per hour?"

"Done! I'll have a copy of the writ and all the evidence we have accumulated so far, sent to you. If you need to read the trial transcripts, I'll make them available. Just let me know."

"Okay. For now, just let me start with the written pleadings."

"By the way, I understand that you are friends with Michael Rawlings? He is now lead counsel for the prosecution."

"Yeah, we became friends after we went against each other before the California Supreme Court. I'll call him and let him know that I'm coming into the case. He's a fair man." Devin thanked him and hung up the phone. He instructed Michelle to deliver a copy of the file to Brent with a check for $7,500.

That afternoon, Jackson Mo came to the office bringing with him six hours of taped interviews of various individuals. He said, "You're going to find these very enlightening. I think it would be easier if I'd just explain the content first and you can transcribe them later." Devin asked him to proceed.

"I spoke first with Miao. He gave names of people who worked for Felix and his late father and who were familiar with Solomon Chin and Frank La. Miao told me that they were all 'made' guys and very well connected and that in order to get me in, he had to clear it with Felix. The following day Miao called me and said it was okay to contact them, that he had Felix's blessing. So, over the next few days I met with six gang members, three who worked for Felix's father back in the day and the others, for Felix. The first meeting was with Alan Chan. He was in his 60's and had been one of the bosses under Felix's dad. He's been retired for a while but still gets gang privileges. He said he remembered Miao's father who worked for Mr. Wong, who was in charge of a couple of the family's restaurants. One day he had reported to Chan

that a couple of managers were stealing money, so Chan reported this to Mr. Wong who banished them from Chinatown. He had thought to have them killed but he was told that they had young children, so he decided not to. It's well known, however, that these two individuals were never able to work again in the Chinese community. He doesn't know what happened to them, but they always blamed Miao's father for their misfortune.

After Wong died, Felix took over the operation and made amends for his father by giving Solomon Chin and Frank La. They were a few years younger than Felix and he kind of took care of them. He didn't know why his dad had banished their fathers. He believed they carried a grudge against Miao's father."

He took a long drink of water and continued with his reporting. "Other interviews corroborated the story. They were also gangsters who work for Wong. I also interviewed Jude Loh and Oscar Ding they work *for Felix and were boyhood friends of Chin and La. They told me that they hated Miao's father for what he did to their fathers and have carried their grudge ever since. They said that they talked about it a lot when they were growing up, but they were kids and couldn't do anything about it. Then when Miao's father died, that's when Mr. Wong took Stephen in like his own son, which multiplied their anger and hatred. This explains their reason for ratting out Miao, to get even for their father's sins."*

Devin sat there listening to Jackson speak, connecting all the dots. When he finished, he asked if any of them would be willing to testify?

They said, *"Only if Felix gives his approval. I think Felix would do that - Stephen and he are like brothers. You didn't hear this from me, but in my opinion, they are partners in crime. It's clear that Felix did not condone their behavior."*

Devin said, "Great work! You deserve a bonus for getting all of this important information."

Mo smiled and bowed a little from the waist, "No, boss. It's my pleasure. We are a team."

Devin felt total relief knowing his gun was now fully loaded. All this information could blow the case sky high. He called Miao and thanked him, telling him he was extremely grateful for providing such useful ammunition, believing it was vital to the case.

Miao replied, "So do I. Please use it wisely. I don't want to go to jail."

"With everything we have, that's very unlikely. Please get me your character witnesses as soon as possible? I want to be ready." Driving home that evening, Devin laughed all the way home. He grabbed his wife and swung her around the room the minute he walked in the door. His wife hadn't seen him in such good spirits for a long time. It felt good.

Game On!!

19

There was never a dull moment at the office. A call came in from Mary Chester, the wife of an old client of Devin's. "Devin, you're not going to believe this!" she almost shouted. "Ralph was driving home from an outing with the boys last night and while he was stopped at a red light, he noticed a very attractive young lady seated at the bus stop!"

Devin said, "Let me guess... he offered her a ride."

"Yes, in his brand-new red Corvette. She told him she was going to San Pedro and, of course, Ralph told her that was his destination, too, to get in the car. When they reached San Pedro she thanked him for the ride by offering him a blow job, so he pulled the car around the corner into a residential neighborhood. This was about 10:30, that's when she went down on him. Can you believe that? What an Asshole?"

Devin wasn't altogether surprised but asked, "How do you know all this, Mary?"

"Because he called me to bail him out of jail, that's how!"

"How did he get arrested? That's bizarre!"

She said that after the blow job, both car doors flew open, it was the police. They had been following the girl and when they saw him park his car, they arrested him for lewd acts on a minor. "But that's not the worst of it, as far as Ralph is concerned. Turns out the girl was really a boy! As pissed off as I was at him, I had to laugh. He didn't think it was one bit funny. Ha!"

Then she asked how she could get him out of jail – this was all new to her. *She wasn't laughing now.*

"Don't worry, Mary. I'll take care of it."

"Thank you. I can't wait for him to come home. How serious is this, Devin?"

"If that girl or boy, was really under age, it could be a felony. We'll need to wait and see, but in the meantime, don't be too hard on him. I'm sure he's panicked thinking he'll never live this down. Where is he being held?"

"At the LAPD station in San Pedro."

Devin explained that after I make the call, he should be released within a couple of hours. "Go pick him up. Do you know what happened to his car?" She replied, "No".

Devin hung up and made the bail arrangements. He had Ray call the San Pedro station to find out what happened to the vehicle and get the names of the arresting officers. *Devin pitied poor Ralph. Mary is going to kill him.*

The following day Ralph called and thanked Devin for bailing him out and swore it was a girl.

"I've spoken to one of the arresting officers," Devin told him, almost kindly. "It was a boy. Lucky for you, he was over 18 years old. You have a court date in three weeks. I'll take care of it. I'm sure the punishment you receive at the hands of Mary, will far exceed anything the court would do to you."

"No shit! Please don't tell anyone, ok?"

"Of course, not. But you must admit, it's kind of funny, don't you think?" *No. Click*

20

Devin and Ray thought it would be a good idea to get Miao's case ready early, thinking the judge would appreciate their thoroughness. Besides, it might give the prosecutor a scare if he thought the case was really going to trial and wouldn't be settled at the last moment, which he knew was the practice of many attorneys.

The witness list included Miao's uncle, his wife, character witnesses, a fingerprint expert and some members of Wong's gang. The subpoenas were prepared for everyone except Miao's wife. Devin wanted them served immediately before anyone 'suddenly' disappeared. The exhibits included financial records, pictures of his business and his home, all to show his standard of living. This was all part of Devin's *'show me the money'* defense strategy. Devin planned to reserve his opening statement, wanting to keep his defense theory under wraps from the prosecutor for as long as possible. Letting it out of the bag sooner would give the prosecutor the opportunity to find evidence to contradict his theory. He wanted to be especially careful to follow the court rules because he knew each jurisdiction was always a little different, particularly in the federal court system where the judge was like an Emperor in his own courtroom.

The trial was a week or so away and the Tanner case was to immediately follow. Ted, Ray and Brent were putting the case together and had informed Devin not to worry, that he would be more than ready. Brent would be acting as lead trial counsel because of his relationship with the opposing attorney, so Devin was free to focus on other matters. He had only one other matter to attend to before starting the Miao trial;
that was the arraignment and plea for Ralph Chester.

The charges were 'lewd acts in a public place', a misdemeanor.

The following morning, he appeared in Department D of the Long Beach Courthouse. The client was told that since it was a misdemeanor charge, he need not be present. The judge in Department D, Richard Travis, happened to be an old high school friend of Devin's. He received the discovery information consisting of the police reports, booking information and a picture of the alleged prostitute. Ralph was right she/ he really looked like a girl. As a girl, she/he was beautiful. She/he would have fooled any normal male. Devin asked for *second call,* which meant that the court would go through its regular calendar before calling Devin's case. He wanted time to speak with the prosecutor about a disposition. David Pettler, the City Attorney, was handling the court calendar. Devin didn't know him. He was an older fellow who probably was a career city attorney who opted for the easiest job which was handling arraignments, requiring very little legal skill.

When the final case was called, the judge took a recess. Devin and Pettler adjourned to a side room adjacent to the courtroom. As they sat down at a small table, Pettler said, "I've seen you around the courthouse. Sorry I haven't had the pleasure to personally meet you."

Devin responded, "Likewise."

"What can I do for you today?"

Devin chose his words carefully. "I'd like you to dismiss the case against my client."

Pettler was surprised by Devin's response. He sized him up and replied matter-of-factly, "No can do. He can plead to the charge, if that's his desire, or plead not guilty; it's only the arraignment."

Devin responded politely, "I know you're a seasoned attorney and you understand that any type of conviction or plea to a sexually-based case, carries with it long-term effects. I would ask you to please read the police reports carefully. You will find that there's nothing in there that confirms anyone saw any type of sexual act being performed, in a public place or otherwise. All a cop saw was the head of the passenger disappearing beneath their sight line, so they assumed the act. In fact, when they opened the cars doors, they saw nothing. Nothing."

After searching Devin's face for a long moment, Pettler said, "Okay, I'll look." Devin walked away giving him time to review the file in private.

Approximately ten minutes later, he said, "Look, maybe you're right, but even if I wanted to, I don't have the authority to dismiss the case.

"Why don't we ask for a bench conference and bring up the question before the judge? Would you agree to dismiss the case if the judge said so?"

Pettler said, "Hey, if that makes you happy. Just know that Judge Travis is a law and order guy and you're not going to get to first base with him."

"Let's at least give it a try, okay?"

Less than twenty minutes later, they were at the bench before Judge Travis, who greeted O'Neill. He responded in kind, and was asked to proceed. He laid out the sordid story, ending with a furrowed brow and a half smile, saying "Your Honor, it's my belief that, for this travesty of justice, the punishment that's been bestowed on him by his wife is far greater than anything the court would do. In fact, she is here in court. She brought my client here, practically by his ear, to face the music. This is not the kind of case where a John is looking for a prostitute. In fact, it's completely the opposite. The problem here is that, as we all know, any type of sex crime carries with it a lifetime of baggage. I'm asking you to recommend a dismissal of this case."

Judge Travis smirked and pondered for a few minutes and then said, "Yes, I suppose I would, if it were up to me."

Pettler was taken aback. He never thought for a second the judge would rule that way. He said, "Your Honor, if you think that little of the case, I'll agree to dismiss it pursuant to Penal Code Section 1385." Devin gave the judge a grateful look as he returned to counsel table.

The City Attorney on record said, "After a bench conference with the court, I'm going to dismiss the case under 1385 of the Penal Code." The judge banged his gavel and approved the case as 'dismissed.'

Devin's stunned client remained in the gallery with his wife, waiting to exit with Devin. As they both followed him out into the hallway, Mary said, "Thank you so much, Devin. We can't thank you enough." He gave her a light hug and turned to Ralph saying,

"Keep it in your pants." *Ralph, looking very uncomfortable, replied, 'thank you'.*

21

Michelle had booked Devin into the Sacramento Sheraton for the following week. On Sunday Devin flew up early, wanting to be prepared for whatever was coming; Ray had driven up a day earlier with all the files. Jackson Mo met Devin at the airport and drove him to the hotel where Ray was waiting. It was early in the evening and they all met in the bar for a drink and to discuss and plan for the next day's events. Wanting to be well rested for the morning meeting, they called it an early evening.

The next morning, they met in the coffee shop to sort out who took what files and plan their arrivals at the courthouse, strategically. It was about a ten-minute walk from the hotel, so Ray, who was responsible for getting the files to court, left a little after nine to clear security. Devin and Jackson followed a half hour later, meeting Miao, his wife and their two children, in front of the courtroom. *Devin hoped the judge would allow the kids to stay in the courtroom, it was good for the jury to see them as a family.* Everyone was a little nervous but, hopefully, that feeling would disappear as soon as the proceedings started.

Eric arrived with Loftin, his investigator, greeting Devin and Ray in front of the courtroom. Arnold walked up to Devin and with a no-nonsense voice, remarked, "Well, this is it. When I go through those doors, all offers are off the table."

Devin thanked him and said, "My client wants his trial, so as Michael Buffer says, *'Let's Get Ready to Rumble!'*

Eric almost hissed, "Your client will be sorry for his decision. Remember that!"

At that point, Devin extended his hand and Arnold shook it. "I guess we've just touched gloves." Arnold just turned away and entered the courtroom.

Ray approached the clerk, filing the proofs of service of the subpoenas; all but four had made on-call arrangements. Devin took his place at counsel table, left of the podium. The prosecutor's table was on the right side, near the jury box and witness stand. *Devin knew that in all courtrooms across the country, this gave the prosecutor more visibility with the jury. That's how the stage was set for justice within a courtroom.*

Miao, his wife and children remained in the hallway at Devin's instructions. Ray verified with the clerk that the court had their witness and exhibit lists, along with a bench copy of the actual exhibits. All seemed in order, then, just before the judge entered the courtroom, Miao came in and whispered in Devin's ear that Chan, Shi, Ding and Loh had just shown up, they were in the hallway.

Devin immediately explained to the clerk that he needed a few minutes before starting because some of the subpoenaed witnesses had just arrived and he needed time with them. Walking out into the hallway with Devin, Miao approached the four very nervous Chinese witnesses. After quick introductions, Miao spoke to them in Chinese for a few minutes, explaining the upcoming events in the courtroom and they seemed to relax. Miao explained why they were there, telling them they could leave after the court started if they promised to return when requested. He assured them there were no tricks and they should follow Devin and Miao back into the courtroom and take a seat in the audience.

Five minutes later, the judge took the bench and asked if everyone was ready. All sides answered, yes. At that point, Devin asked the court for permission to allow his client's wife and children to remain during the trial. The judge responded yes, they're welcome to stay if they behave. Devin then advised Judge Garcia that four witnesses who were under subpoena had arrived and were seated in the audience. Devin asked each one to stand and state their name, explaining to the court that he was willing to place them on call since he didn't believe he would need their testimony for a few days. They had all promised to return to court if summoned, within a 24-hour notice.

Arnold gave each witness a hard look of disapproval. The judge said, "Okay, I'll excuse them and order them to return to this courtroom within 24 hours of receiving your telephone call." They all agreed, leaving their cell phone numbers with Devin. They were gone in a flash. *Devin was very pleased that they showed up - they were going to play a big role in trashing the prosecution's witnesses.*

After some brief court business, a jury panel was brought in and by 4 o'clock that afternoon, they were impaneled. *Sadly, the jury selection simply did not represent a jury of Miao's peers... there was not one*

Asian to be seen. The trial was going to start in earnest the following morning.

Once all the players were in place the next day, the prosecution called its first witness, real estate broker, Julie Chen, to establish that she had sold the properties where the marijuana was discovered. She ID'd the buyers and testified that, although she had seen Miao on a couple of occasions, she had no dealings with him. On cross examination, she explained that he had accompanied one of the buyers a couple of times and she was told that he was a contractor who might possibly do some remodeling for the buyer. *Devin thought she was harmless.*

The next witness was Mrs. Wallace, a neighbor who had reported her observations about one of the houses, to the police. *No, she never saw Miao.*

Dan McFarland, one of the investigators, testified that he was the person who searched the records and determined that the 20 houses in question were acquired by the same two companies. He stated that he'd observed all 20 of the houses and noted their similarities. Later he had obtained a search warrant for the houses and participated in the searches.

Next, Arnold advised the court that he wanted to show exhibits 20 through 40, videos taken at each house while the searches were taking place. The judge motioned approval and he proceeded, starting with Exhibit 20 on a big screen. He had set it up with the witness, who was describing, in detail, what was being shown to the jury. The one video lasted over 20 minutes; the procedure for the next five videos was to be the same. The judge kept looking at Devin hoping he would object. Devin sat there silently, sometimes scanning the jury, noticing that they were bored and almost falling asleep, along with everyone else in the courtroom, except Loftin and Arnold. After more than two long hours of redundant videos, the judge said in a very exasperated voice, "Mr. Arnold, please don't tell me you're going to show 15 more videos to the jury of the same thing?"

Arnold was startled at the tone from the judge. "Yes, Your Honor. I believe that..."

"No, you're not!" the judge almost shouted. "It's cumulative and a total waste of the court's time!"

Looking directly at O'Neill, he exclaimed, "Mr. O'Neill, would you agree to put us out of our misery by stipulating that all 15 videos represent the same thing the first five did?"

Smiling to himself and taking the judge's glare seriously, O'Neill responded in a calm, cool voice, "Of course, Your Honor. It would be my pleasure."

The judge turned to his clerk, forgetting to turn off his mic, said in a loud whisper heard by the whole courtroom, "Couldn't the US Attorney's office find a more competent attorney to try this case? Good grief!"

For a moment, Devin felt bad for Eric, thinking to himself, *he really should have put together a 10-minute collage representing the searches of all houses, but he didn't. Oh, well – tough shit, pal*!

That ended the day. No damage done. Devin knew things were going to pick up in the days to follow. During the next couple of days, DEA Agent David Loftin, testified as to the amount of marijuana crop growing in each of the houses; in his opinion, they would be able to harvest three crops a year. He was proud of his expertise and tooted his horn for over an hour and, in fact, stated that this was one of the largest busts of marijuana-growing facilities in his career. He opined that the annual income that could be generated by sales of the marijuana would be between $80 to$100 million. *BLah... bLah...bLah.*

Devin sat in silence, knowing this was playing directly into his defense of *'show me the money'*. On cross exam, Loftin re-emphasized and actually embellished that figure to be much closer to $100 million. Devin's final question to him was 'Did you know Miao?' He said no, only through what other witnesses had told him. Devin jumped to objection, citing 'what other people had told him' as hearsay. The judge instructed the jury to disregard what Loftin had just said.

The next witness testified that they had lifted a fingerprint which belonged to Miao, from the garage of one of the houses. *Devin thought an explanation for that could easily be explained later.*

"Can you tell the jury when that fingerprint was specifically put there? *No idea.* "Did you find any other fingerprints of my client at any of the other 20 houses?" *No.*

It was Friday afternoon and everyone was excused until Monday. Devin was sure that would be when Chin and La would claim that Miao was the boss and ring leader of their criminal enterprise. He was more than ready for them. Bring it on!

He flew home looking forward to a relaxing weekend at the beach with his family. They were always his safe harbor.

22

Devin arrived at the courthouse early on Monday morning. He was ready for action. As Solomon Chin reached the witness box, Devin whispered to Stephen to stare him down. Chin caught the action and looked nervous. *Devin knew he was about to lie through his teeth so he looked intently at him, hoping he stayed nervous throughout his testimony.*

The beginning was mundane, talking about his early years, his family, schooling, etc. Then it really started. When he was in high school, Felix Wong had offered him a job at one of the restaurants, starting in the kitchen, working his way up to waiter and finally, assistant manager. That's when he said he first became acquainted with Stephen Miao, who seemed to be a close friend of Felix. At first, it was just to say hello, then one day Stephen asked him if he wanted to make some extra money. He said of course... what do

I have to do? Stephen told him that he owned a bunch of houses in the Sacramento area which he used to grow marijuana and that the crop was harvested 2 to 3 times a year. That all he had to do was to go to the houses, pack up the marijuana and transport it to his warehouse in San Francisco. He would be provided with the transportation and would be paid one thousand dollars per trip. Admitting that he was impressed with the money he could make, he had agreed to do it and that's how he had gotten involved. He explained that Felix did not know of the arrangement with Miao. Then he testified that he'd made between 20 to 30 runs before getting arrested. He told the jury he was sorry for what he had done. That knowing now what he'd gotten himself into, he seriously regretted it.

Arnold said, no more questions, and took his seat. Having paid close attention to the details of the testimony, Devin had chosen not to object to *anything... let him dig a hole so deep that he can't climb out of it.*

As Devin approached, he stood at the podium and in a clear, stern voice said, "Mr. Chin, can you tell the jury why you have just lied to all of us about Stephen Miao?"

Arnold was about to object but sat down. Chin's eyes darted left and right, like a trapped animal. "I didn't lie! It's the truth."

Devin continued, "How did you meet Felix Wong?"

"I was in high school looking for a job at a restaurant in Chinatown. As it turned out, it was owned by Felix Wong."

"Had you ever heard of him before?" *No.*

"Didn't your father work for King Wong, Felix's father?" *I don't know that.* "Didn't your father tell you he was fired from his job by Felix's father?" *No.* "Isn't it true that you met Felix for the first time when he was a teenager at the restaurant where your father was working?" *No.* "And that's when you first met Stephen Miao, Felix's friend." *No.*

"Solomon, where's your father now?" *I don't know.* "Wasn't he banished, along with Frank La's father, from Chinatown by Felix's father, for stealing money?" *I don't know.*

At this point, Eric objected as to relevancy. Devin replied, "Your Honor, it's foundational to impeach the veracity of this witness." The judge motioned approval to keep going.

"Your father was banished and never allowed to work again in Chinatown. That really hurt your family finances, didn't it?" *I don't know what you're talking about.* "You were aware that Felix's father was head of the Chinese Wah Lo Gang in San Francisco, weren't you?"

Objection! That assumes a fact not in evidence. Sustained. Next question, Mr. O'Neill.

"You and Frank La blamed Stephen's father for ratting them out and getting them fired, didn't you?" *No. I don't know what you are talking about.* "Do you know Jude Loh?" *Yes.* "Didn't you tell him that you were going to avenge your father's firing by getting even with the Miao family?" *No.* "Do you know Brian Lee… again, asking the same question?"

Devin then went through the questioning of each of his impeaching witnesses, putting forth the same questions. *The answer was always the same, no.*

"And when Stephen's father died, you transferred your hatred to Stephen, didn't you?" *No, that's not true.* "Didn't you tell Alvin Chan that you were going to get even with Stephen Miao because you couldn't go after his dead father?" *The answer was the same, no.*

By now Chin was squirming in his chair, his slicked black hair falling on his forehead, sweaty. Devin continued the pounding. "Felix's father died, do you recall that?" *Yes*. "And that's when you and La were still in high school, correct?" *Yes*. "Isn't that when Felix approached you and offered you a job since he had now taken over his father's businesses?" *I don't remember*. "And that's when you started not only working in the restaurants, but you also became a member of the Wah Lo Gang, which was now headed up by Felix, since his father's death." *No*. "Mr. Chin, would you please roll up the sleeve on your right arm?" *Why?* Arnold objected.

"Your Honor, I believe we will all see Chinese characters tattooed there. I have a gang expert here who will testify that those symbols represent a membership in the Wah Lo Gang." The judge asked Chin to roll up his sleeve. He stood at the witness chair and took off his jacket, rolling up his sleeve. A large, colorful tattoo with distinctive Chinese characters were clearly visible on his upper arm.

Devin pointed to the tattoo and asked, "What is that?" *A tattoo.* "Don't get cute with me, Mr. Chin. We all know it's a tattoo. Could you tell us what it represents?"

"Okay, okay! I'm in a Chinese gang, so what?" Chin tried to look indignant.

Devin walked up close to him and asked, "Why did you just lie and say you weren't?" *I don't know.* "Your friend La is also a gang member, true?" *Yes.* "And Felix Wong is your boss?" *Yes.* "And you wouldn't do anything without his okay, would you?" *No.* "Do you know Felix's whereabouts?" *Yes, he's in China.* "Do you know when he went there?" *I think it was just after we got arrested.*

Devin walked slowly to his table, mostly for effect as he turned toward the jury, "As a member of

Wah Lo, you needed Felix's approval to work outside of gang activities or face death, isn't that true?" *Yes, that's true.* "So, let me understand, you told us that you didn't tell Felix about this, but you are still alive. Why?" *No answer. His silence was deafening.* "Is that because you never really worked for my client, Mr. Chin?" *No, I did.*

"The people working in the marijuana houses, they were your gang buddies, correct?" *Could be.* "How about the people working at the warehouse on the pier? They were gang members also, weren't they?" *Don't know.* "When you got arrested, you wanted to cooperate, didn't you?" *Yes.* "Did you give those individuals' names to the police?" *No.* Is that because they were your gang brothers? But you gave up Miao, didn't you?" *Objection, Your Honor.*

Devin kept his back to Chin as he said, "I withdraw the question, Your Honor. I have just one more question... what did the prosecution offer you to testify against my client?" *Nothing, only that they would advise the court of my cooperation when it came time for me to be sentenced.*

"Thank you. No more questions."

Arnold rose and stood at the podium in silence until the judge jumped in and said, "Mr. Arnold, do you have any questions for the witness?"

"Sorry, your honor. I was just thinking."

"Well, let's get on with it!" the judge exclaimed.

At this point, Arnold said, "Mr. Chin, before you agreed to testify, you signed a plea agreement, right?" *Yes.* Arnold approached the witness and handed him a written plea agreement. *Chin acknowledged it.* "You promised to tell the truth. Did you tell the truth here, today?" *Yes, to the best of my ability.* "So, whether you are a gang member or not, was Stephen Miao the person you were working for in the marijuana business?" *Yes.* Devin thought that *it was a feeble attempt to re-habilitate poor Solomon Chin.*

It was near the afternoon recess, Arnold asked for sidebar. He explained to the judge that he was surprised by Chin's testimony and asked for a day off to investigate and prepare his other witnesses, based upon the accusations during Mr. O'Neill's cross examination.

Devin objected, saying the prosecutor had months to prepare their case. "I can't help it if their witness was lying!"

The judge said, "I agree, Mr. O'Neill, but I was going to cut the afternoon session off early due to a judge's meeting and was going to be dark tomorrow, anyway. So, Mr. Arnold, you got your extra time, put it to good use." *Devin knew the cops would be checking out all his witnesses' backgrounds, but it was of no use.*

It was incredibly fortunate that the gang tattoo information had come to him by a comment made in passing, by Alvin Chan. Devin didn't give it much thought at the time, however, he had asked Miao if *he* had any gang tattoos. He'd explained that he didn't have any because Felix had kept him out of it. *Devin knew that would play well with the jury's 'show and tell'.*

The break was welcome. Devin got to see a little of the Capitol, feeling a bit like a tourist. A couple of days later, when the hearing re-convened, Frank La took the stand. He was less prepared than Chin, however, he was coached enough to stick to his story. He admitted to being a gang member and testified that Felix was the man in charge but otherwise, he denied all the allegations put forth by Devin, especially his revenge theory, as the reason for pointing the finger at Miao. The prosecutor rested his case after La.

After lunch recess, Devin made his opening statement by using his well-planned *"SHOW ME THE MONEY"* strategy. It started with Stephen's life as a child, through his teenage years, his schooling, his relationship with his family; explaining that his father worked for Felix Wong's father in his restaurants in Chinatown; that being an honest, loyal employee, when he had caught Chin's and La's fathers stealing money, he reported them to Felix's father, which resulted in their being banished permanently from Chinatown. Then when his father died, Felix's father took him in as a son. He told how Stephen and Felix were close friends all the way through school and in college; going their separate ways in business, but remaining close, social friends. He knew that Felix took over the family businesses after his father had died and, like his father before him, was a gang member. Miao, on the other hand, was never a gang member.

He outlined that La and Chin's friends and fellow gang members, would testify that they hated Stephen Miao's father for turning their fathers in many years ago. That they wanted to exact revenge and since Stephen's father was dead, they directed their vindications toward Stephen; testifying against him. They would see that there was no way, as a loyal gang member, that they would they have involved themselves in the marijuana business unless it was part of a gang enterprise.

He concluded his presentation statement with a long, deliberate look at the jury members. "Ladies and gentlemen of the jury, after you have heard all the evidence, there will be only one verdict you can reach - and that's, NOT GUILTY. Thank you.

Devin's first witness was Stephen's wife. She followed the script perfectly, crying at the appropriate times. *She gave a heart-wrenching description of her life, immigrating with her parents as a young child from*

China, only to lose them both in a car accident when she was only 12. Thereafter, she was raised by her grandparents who never learned a word of English. She met Stephen in her first year at San Francisco State. They were married right after graduation and started a family. She handled all the family finances while Stephen worked hard to support their family, always giving her his paychecks. She described their lifestyle, which included raising the children, plus, taking care of her elderly grandfather who lived with them. They seldom took vacations except to take the children to Disneyland or family-friendly places like that. There was very little left after the bills were paid, so on special occasions, they sometimes had dinner with Felix at one of his restaurants; since Stephen and Felix were close childhood friends, growing up together. She couldn't recall, however, if Felix ever visited their home nor If they visited his. She authenticated their tax returns, bank records, financial statements and loan applications used to finance the purchase of their home and/or occasional vehicle. Their lifestyle was that of a typical middle-class family, as shown in the pictures of their home. Devin could not have been happier with her testimony.

Arnold tried to get her to say that her husband was in business with Felix, which fell flat on its face. He asked her if she knew Solomon Chin or Frank La. *She said no, the first time she knew they ever existed was when they testified in court the other day.* He asked her about the SUV. *She said it was her grandfather's... that he used it occasionally to take the kids to their public school before she got her driver's license.* Arnold asked about her grandfather's whereabouts. *She explained that he went to China to attend to a sick relative; that to pay for the trip, he sold the SUV.*

Nothing was going right for Arnold. The picture he was trying to paint turned out to be a blank canvas. He attempted to show that Stephen spent days and nights away from the home. *She said he was only gone on days when he went to work, which was usually six days a week; but he always came home for dinner with the family.* Completely frustrated, Arnold pointed an accusatory finger at her, "You would say anything to protect your husband, wouldn't you?" Even lie for him?"

Refusing to be intimidated, her response was classic, "In my culture we are told never to lie, so no, I wouldn't."

As Arnold walked away from the podium he said in a loud, sarcastic voice, "Of course, you would!" *The strategy was working. 'Show me the money' was right on track.*

Stephen's uncle testified that Stephen was a partner in his contracting business. They mainly did remodeling, specializing in kitchens and bathrooms. He told them that *the business was good. Most of the houses in the San Francisco area were older and always in need of updating.* To help verify the legitimacy of the contracting business, Devin showed some pictures of their place of business and some of the houses they had remodeled.

Finally, Devin said, "I don't wish to pry into your finances, but I have five years of your business tax returns and I am asking the Judge for permission to show them for verification." Continuing his 'show and tell' for the jury, he read from the document… "*In its best year, these show earnings of $220,000, before taxes and assets such as tools, trucks and supplies, totaling $175,000. Are those figures, correct? No fudging?"*

"No fudging," his uncle replied. "They are to the penny."

On cross, Arnold asked what Miao's responsibilities were? The witness replied, *"He bids jobs, supervises workers and gets down on his hands and knees and does the labor. He's a good, hard-working boy."* Then he asked about Sam Woo.

Uncle said, "He has been a family friend for many years, he owns a hardware store in Marin County. I purchase all my supplies from him." Do you know where he is now? *"I was told that he went to China. All I know is that he shut down his business. I was sad about that because I could never beat his prices."* So far, Devin was batting a thousand.

Arnold then asked, "Do you know Felix Wong?" *Yes, of course. Felix's father was a big shot in Chinatown. My brother worked for him and when he died, Felix's father took Stephen in as his own son. Stephen and Felix were tight friends all through school, as I remember.* "How would you describe their relationship now?" *I can't really answer that. I haven't seen Felix for over five years. You'll need to ask them.* "Did your company do any remodeling jobs for Felix?" *Not that I'm aware of.* "Did you do any remodeling jobs in the Sacramento area?" *No, that would be out of our territory.* "To your knowledge, did Stephen ever bid any construction jobs out of town for Felix or for anyone else?" *Not that I'm aware of, you would need to ask him. We could never afford to do jobs that far away.* Arnold continued, "Are you aware that your nephew, Stephen Miao, is on trial for dealing drugs?" *Yes, but it must be a joke. He's as straight as an arrow.*

Arnold shook his head, looking toward the jury and commented, "I guess families stick together," loud enough for the jury to hear.

Devin jumped up and asked the court to strike the comment, exclaiming, "That remark implies that the witness is lying!"

The judge said, "Yes, it's stricken. Mr. Arnold's comments are not evidence. Please disregard them. And you, Mr. Arnold, keep your comments to yourself!"

Devin knew that to win the case, he had to destroy Solomon Chin and Frank La. The next four witnesses, Alvin Chan, Jude Loh, Brian Lee and Oscar Ding were crucial to the case; depending on how they testified... would tell the whole story. They were admitted gang members in the Wah Lo organization. They knew both, Chin and La, as gang brothers, and were familiar with the history concerning their fathers and Felix's father. Devin wanted to bring out each one's criminal history before cross examination by Arnold, who would surely bring it up. They were also aware that when Felix took over as head of the organization, he had brought Chin and La into the fold. *Hold your breath...*

They testified that Stephen Miao was a close friend of Felix and, as far as they knew, he was not a gang member. Nor to their knowledge, did he participate in any of their gang activities. They all testified about the conversations they had with Chin and La about their hatred for the Miao family, blaming them for their own fathers' downfall. They further claimed no knowledge of growing marijuana. Jude Loh was the only one who took the fifth when that issue arose. They all agreed that they do not 'rat out' their gang members - if they did, it was a death sentence.

"How about ratting out a non-gang member? Would it be okay?" *That would be all right.* "Would it be permissible to work outside of the gang?" *No, was the answer. They could not think of an exception.* "How many gang members are there?" *Hundreds, that they knew about. The gang started in mainland China and Taiwan way back, and now has activities in many states across the country.* "So, it's possible that gang activity such as cultivating marijuana in the Sacramento area, could be happening without you knowing about it?" *Yes.* Devin thought he should quit while he was ahead. No more questions.

Arnold was at his best. He pointed out that they did not know whether Chin or La, did or didn't, work for Miao, or that the reasons for ratting him out was to avenge their families' disgrace. They all agreed that if they worked for Miao they would have needed Felix's okay; that he would need to ask Felix himself, about that, but since they were living and breathing they assumed Felix could have easily given them consent.

Devin felt the door opening by the cross examination; he needed to close it quickly, but he had to tread lightly. He asked about their knowledge of gang life. Had any gang member gone off the reservation, so to speak? *All answered, no.* Had their boss ever given consent to any gang member to 'moonlight'? *Not to their knowledge.* "So, it would be unlikely that Chin or La would have operated outside of the gang?" *They all agreed.*

Arnold jumped in and asked, "But it's possible, isn't it?"

Devin objected, "Anything is possible! The question is asking the witness to speculate."

Arnold said, "Withdrawn." He obviously just wanted to plant the idea in the jury's minds. The court recessed for the day.

Devin, Ray and Jackson had an early dinner at *Lilies*, a restaurant they'd discovered around the corner from the hotel. The food was good and the privacy was conducive to their needs, so it became their un-official headquarters every evening after court.

This evening was extra important. They needed to make a decision about Miao, who was to be their last witness. Did they need him? The bigger question was, did the jury want to hear from him; that he was not involved? Devin thought that would be the only reason to put him on, otherwise, the case looked pretty good as it stood.

Ray raised a good point. "Maybe the jury thinks that Felix was Miao's silent partner, and that's why some of the gang members were involved in the criminal enterprise. That would also explain why our client did not show any money, because Felix was holding it for him."

Devin sat up, slapping Ray on the back. "I didn't think of that! Way to go, Ray. I wonder if Arnold thought of it?" He leaned back into the booth, smiling, confident and finally, relaxed. "So that's it! Stephen Miao **must** testify to clear up that crucial, unanswered question."

Devin called Stephen from the restaurant and asked him to meet him at his hotel at eight the following morning to discuss his upcoming testimony. Miao was confused and said, "I thought I wasn't going to have to testify?"

Devin responded, "I think the jury needs to hear from you directly, so I need to prep you. Please have your character witnesses available to be in court tomorrow, I'll see you in the morning."

Devin had a couple of glasses of wine with dinner, enjoying the conversation with Ray and Jackson, forgetting the case for a few minutes. Thank God it would all be over very soon. The focus was a burnout, but he felt good about the case. He called his wife and told her he would be home by tomorrow night, if everything went as planned. *People think it's glamorous to travel and be away from home, doing trials, but it's not, it's like being a fish out of water. At the end of the day, it's like Dorothy says, 'there is no place like home.'*

Devin could not sleep that night even after taking a hit on a joint (*he thought, there is no crime in it unless you get caught, of course.*) He was planning his closing argument in his head. He always thought that his subconscious was smarter than his conscious; that he had his best ideas from his dreamy state of mind. He finally fell asleep, trying to find his 'dreamy' stage.

He felt fresh and rested when he awoke. He even sang in the shower, calmly ignoring the fact that he had a terrible voice. He met Miao and his wife in the hotel lobby coffee shop where they took time for some coffee and English muffins. He proceeded to explain the necessity of calling him as a witness to dispel any idea that he and Felix were partners. "I'm concerned that if the prosecution is smart enough to think of this, it could hurt our

'show me the money' defense. The fact that your wife's grandfather, Mr. Woo, and Felix, suddenly went to China

after the drug bust, could carry serious weight. Let's not let that happen, Stephen. Convince them that you were set up as a scapegoat."

Stephen nodded in understanding, "I'm ready. I have nothing to hide." Devin thought Miao looked good in his new suit and tie as he walked over to the court house.

Ready for action, Devin directed his remarks to the judge, "Your Honor, our next witness is Stephen Miao." Stephen rose from counsel table and walked confidently in front of all the jurors to the witness box, with all eyes upon him. The clerk gave him the oath. Devin wanted his testimony to be short and smart. As the questions flowed, Stephen followed Devin's instructions to a tee. He looked into the eyes of each juror as he answered the questions. Finally, it was time to ask about his relationship with Felix, when and where it had started. *He explained that they were boyhood friends and when his father died, he moved in with Felix's family because his mother returned to China to be with her relatives. All the way through high school they were like brothers, after high school they both went to San Francisco State University. While there, Felix's father died and Felix dropped out of school and took over his father's business. After that, their relationship began to fade. Stephen continued his college education, they only spoke a couple of times a month and, before long, they hardly spoke at all, except for sharing an occasional dinner. Although Felix was best man at his wedding, Stephen got the feeling that Felix didn't want to be seen in his new role as head of a criminal enterprise, so he respected his need for privacy. However, on rare occasions, Felix would refer business to him. He had even asked Stephen to help remodel part of Felix's personal home and once asked for his help inspecting some of his friends' properties who were thinking of buying in the Sacramento area. Stephen said that when he got arrested, it took him by surprise. He had no explanation as to why Solomon Chin or Frank La had lied about his involvement.*

"Have you ever been in business with Felix?" *The answer was no.* "Have you ever been involved in the cultivation and distribution of marijuana?" *Never.* "When was the last time you, either, spoke to or saw Felix Wong?" *Maybe a year ago.* "Do you know where he is now?" *No.* "Are you a member of Wah Lo Gang?" *No.* "Or any gang, for that matter?" *Never!*

Arnold was anxious to start his cross examination. "Does your wife's grandfather own an SUV?" *Yes.* "Do you know how old he is?" *I think he's in his middle to Late 60's.* "I understand he lives with you in your home?" *He did until recently when he returned to China to attend a dying relative.* "What kind of work does he do?" *He's retired.* "From what?" *He owned a Chinese Laundry.* (laughter from the jury) "Did you buy him the SUV?" *Yes.* "Why?" *Because at the time my wife did not have a driver's license and she needed to get around, kids to school, shopping, etc. I was always at work, so Henry was her driver. I also paid for his insurance. When my wife got* her license, I told him to keep the SUV for himself. "Where is it now?" *It's my understanding he sold it to pay for his trip to China.* "Was he involved with Felix or his father?" *He knew the Wong family since his business was in Chinatown. Everyone knew Felix's dad.* "Is your wife's grandfather a Wah Lo gang member?" *No.* "Did you use the SUV to transport marijuana from houses in Sacramento?" *No, never.* "Did you give the SUV to others to transport marijuana?" *Never.*

Arnold's questions changed. He asked Stephen about Sam Woo. Stephen told him that he met Woo through his uncle who supplied tools, construction equipment and other items for their business; that he had no other contact with him. "Is Woo a gang member, to your knowledge?" *I have no idea.* "Do you know where Woo is now?" *No.* The questions turned to Stephen's fingerprints in the grow houses. Stephen explained why they might have been there, but denied the accusation that he was involved.

Arnold's voice and tone shifted. "Mr. Miao, you and Felix are partners in the cultivation and distribution of marijuana, aren't you?" *Absolutely not.* "And he ran off to China leaving your holding the bag." *Not true.* "If he's in China, as you say, I don't know why. Do you?" Arnold was getting nowhere with his questions and Stephen was coming across cool and collected.

Suddenly, Arnold asked, "Is your cell phone number area code 415-678-4210?" *Miao replied, yes.* Can you please explain the four telephone outgoing calls from your phone to a phone number in China?" Oh shit, Devin thought to himself. *Yes, my wife used my phone to call her grandfather.* Devin relaxed a bit, but knew that Stephen really had communicated with Felix during this time and had no idea what was coming next, especially if they could find who the number belonged to in China. That could blow up his whole case! To Devin's relief Arnold said, no more questions.

When Miao sat down next to Devin at counsel table he whispered in his ear, 'you need to know that those calls were really to Felix.' Devin replied under his breath, "I didn't hear that. Quick thinking, though."

Both sides rested. The judge scheduled the review of the jury instructions for the afternoon, with closing arguments from Monday, giving the jurors a day and a half off. *Devin's defense was still viable, a multimillion dollar business, as so described by the prosecution. So, if Miao was involved, prove it. Show Me the Money!*

Devin polished his closing argument over the weekend. It was late Saturday when he called a couple of friends to have dinner with him and his wife at his favorite restaurant, The Palm, in West Hollywood. During dinner, they quizzed him about his latest case. Devin changed the subject, he had a steadfast rule of never mixing business with personal family or friends time. In fact, most of his friends were not in the legal profession. It just made it easier that way. Much easier.

On Sunday when he arrived back in Sacramento, Jackson was waiting for him at the hotel. Ray did not make the trip. Ted needed him at the office. After a quick review of Monday's court procedures, he called it a night and watched an old war movie, dozing off part-way through. He felt relaxed and confident.

Arnold was first to argue. He was very convincing as he hammered away at the relationship between Felix and Miao, pointing out the closeness between the two; *showing that Felix, who was an admitted gangster and involved in the marijuana business, had his gang brothers also actively involved in the business; highlighting that Miao's fingerprints were found at a couple of the locations, thus, providing evidence of his involvement. Further, he was trying to show that Woo, being the supplier of equipment to grow the marijuana and the supplier for Miao's construction business, was no coincidence, by any means. That, plus, the fact that when the arrests went down, Woo ran off to China and closed his business, was a clear indication of his guilt, also, not a coincidence. Adding to that, Miao's wife's grandfather owned an SUV used by the drug traffickers, and around the time arrests were being made, it was suddenly sold and conveniently disappeared before the police could investigate. Just a coincidence? Not on your life! I submit to you that there is one common thread to all those coincidences - that thread is Stephen Miao! The defense will tell you that Chin and La gave up their client because he was not a gang member. They also argue that they testified against him because of some revenge theory, but neither theory holds water. They have denied that claim. They freely admitted their involvement in the drug business which was for the benefit of their gang and worked at Miao's direction. It's that plain and simple. So, where's the money, the defense will argue? The answer is, Felix is holding it for him! This criminal enterprise required skill and a cool hand to make it happen. You saw Stephen Miao testify in a cool and skillful manner, just exactly like how he ran the drug business for*

Felix. He spun around, looking at Miao, exhorting to the jury what he truly believed. *"He is guilty, Ladies and gentlemen. There is no other story that makes any sense! Therefore, I ask you to connect all the dots… to find him guilty on all charges."* Arnold faced the jury as he thanked them, then walked back to his table with a slight grin on his face. He was sure he'd done his job well.

The judge had given each side one hour for their argument. Arnold took his allotted time. Devin was impressed by his presentation, however, he believed that he was a better artist *(at spinning a story)* and that he had the right chemistry to turn the jury. The clock said 11:05 and Devin didn't want to start his closing argument until after lunch. He wanted as much time to pass as possible. He wanted the jury to forget some of Arnold's presentation, particularly the *'connect the dots'* part. He asked the judge for delay to start, reasoning that he did not want his closing to be interrupted by a lunch recess. The judge understood, however, before making his ruling he asked if the jury would they be willing to delay their lunch recess until after Mr. O'Neill finished his closing remarks. They weren't, Devin got his wish. *Whew.*

Everyone was back in their seats by 1:30. Walking around the courtroom from the podium to the front of the jury box, Devin's voice was slow and deliberate as he began. Making sure their eyes were following him, he stopped on occasion, picked out a juror and directed his gaze to that individual, as if having a personal conversation with him or her, although he was speaking to the entire panel. He did this to each one throughout his remarks, holding their attention. He pointed out that Miao's lifestyle had not changed from before, during or after the alleged criminal activity. *We do not dispute that Miao was a friend of Felix Wong, even a very close friend at one time, but he was not a gang member like his friend, Felix. If he was involved with Felix in his drug business, ask yourselves why wouldn't he have enjoyed the fruits of his relationship with him, the reason is because he had nothing to do with*

Felix's criminal activities. He was a hard-working family man not a gangster; if he were involved, **show me the money**? His home is modest, he makes just enough to pay his bills, He worked hard to get his college degree and, after that, he went into business with his uncle. Why would he do all that if he was in business with Felix? He didn't, because he wasn't! My client told you that Felix took over his *father's family business when Felix's father died; it was at a time when they were both in college. Felix dropped out of school and their friendship drifted apart. Ladies and gentlemen, there is no evidence to the contrary. The prosecution wants you to believe that the SUV that was used to transport marijuana was the one my client bought for his wife's grandfather to drive his family around. There are thousands of black SUV's in the streets of Northern California. There is no evidence that it's the same vehicle. They want you to believe that my client's wife's grandfather disposed of the SUV to avoid attention. I submit to you that he needed the funds to travel to China, *so he sold it. The truth is that, if my client was involved in a hundred-million-dollar drug business, he could have easily sprung for an airline ticket to get him out of town...so again I ask,* **show me the money**!

Devin walked closer to the jury, looked at all of them deliberately, and continued. *He didn't do that. Why? Because the story put forth by the prosecution is a myth. Remember, it's the prosecution's burden to prove their case beyond a reasonable doubt. The prosecution wants you to make an impossible jump by concluding that my client is, somehow, connected to the illegal activities of Woo. Their reasoning is that since Miao's uncle does business with him for their contracting business, that they must know about Woo supplying equipment to grow Marijuana. My client said he knew Woo vaguely as a source of supplies for his uncle's business. Innuendo at best! Again, the prosecution is grasping at straws; that's not evidence of Miao's involvement. To the contrary, he had a legitimate business relationship with Woo's hardware store. We are not saying that Woo is not guilty; that's probably why he ran away, but that has nothing to do with my client.*

The judge will instruct you as to the law and you must follow those instructions. The law states that if certain facts point to one's guilt and also points to innocence, you must adopt the one that points to innocence. I submit to you that everything you have heard over the last couple of weeks, points to my client's innocence. *So, ask yourself why Solomon Chin and Franklin La, who have admitted their involvement in the illegal business of growing Marijuana and being gang members in Felix Wong's gang, would state that Stephen Miao was the person in charge? Wouldn't they lie because they needed to protect the person they were really working for, Felix Wong? Stephen Miao was expendable; it would have been easy to say Felix was the master mind, however, he's long gone to China. They needed to sell out someone to the police so they could get a deal for themselves! There was no mileage in ratting out Felix. The cops already knew that he was involved, besides, ratting out Felix would've been a death warrant. It's easy to see why they picked on Stephen; they didn't like him anyway, plus, it served another purpose - to avenge their father's banishment from Chinatown. It was a win-win for them.*

You also need to ask yourselves, 'how trustworthy are they'? The answer is, 'they are not'. One more thing to factor in; the fingerprint evidence has clearly been explained, so that part is not helpful in your deliberations.

Devin stopped his pacing, lowered his voice, hoping for a serious (*dramatic*) effect as he said, "Do the right thing. Your verdict can only be *not guilty*. Thank you for listening to me."

The jury got the case after the judge read them the instructions. They filed out of the courtroom at 3:30 pm and were told to pick a foreperson. The judge told Devin he needed to be available within 15 minutes, if necessary.

Devin had no idea how long this was going to take so he called Michelle and told her he would wait around for one day, but if the jury was not back by then, she needed to send Ray to take his place for the decision.

That night Devin, Jackson, Stephen and his wife had dinner at Lilie's, a favorite nearby restaurant. They were all optimistic and Devin had more than his share of wine. It had been a long day and before long, he excused himself and returned to the hotel, where he slept like a baby.

The following day no verdict had been reached and Devin thought that was a good sign. He flew back to LA, leaving Jackson and Ray behind to keep Stephen company. Devin kept busy at the office but his mind was on Sacramento. Three days later the judge called everyone back into his courtroom, announcing that he was going to question the jury as to their progress.

It was just before lunch when the jury entered the courtroom. Juror #4 was the foreman. The judge questioned him as to their progress in reaching a decision. The foreman said, "Your honor, we were in the process of writing you a note to explain why we can't reach a unanimous decision."

The judge asked, "If I send you back, do you think your situation might change"

Juror #4 said, no. The judge asked each juror if they concurred with the foreman. The answer was yes. At this point, they were divided 7 for 'not guilty' and 5 for 'guilty.'

"In that case, I'm going to declare a mistrial and excuse you with the court's thanks."

Once the jury left the courtroom, the judge asked Arnold for the US Attorney's position. He replied, "I need to discuss the matter with my superiors, Your Honor."

Judge Garcia said, "During the trial, I listened intently to the evidence and, in my opinion, you will *never* get a unanimous decision. I think your office should seriously consider dismissing the case; I want to know your office's decision this afternoon." With that, he stood up and said, "Everyone be back in my court at 1:30." He left the room.

Ray was all smiles. Stephen didn't understand. Leaving the courtroom, he explained, "It's a big win! The judge will probably dismiss the case if the prosecution wants another trial!" As soon as Ray was in the hallway, he telephoned Devin and gave him the blow-by-blow of the decision.

Devin let out a big sigh of relief, knowing it could have gone either way. He really liked Arnold's closing argument. Jackson and Miao were confused, asking if they were going to have to do this all over again? Ray explained that it was possible, possible but not probable. "The US Attorney usually wins. At this point, this is unfamiliar territory for them. I don't think they want to risk another failure, so they probably will let sleeping dogs lie."

By 2 o'clock, it was all over. The US Attorney decided not to retry the case. Jackson called Devin and thanked him profusely. *This decision would elevate his status in the Chinese community.*

The following morning a package for Devin arrived at the office. He took it into his office and opened it. There was $50,000 in hundred dollar bills! Smiling to himself, he called Ray into the office and gave him $10,000, asking him to keep it under his hat. Ray stared at the cash and with a low whistle said, "Wow! I guess he showed **us** the money!"

23

Ted said, "Congratulations, Devin. Another one bites the dust. But, sorry, no break for you. We are having a big problem with Knowles and Thompson. Their response to our subpoenas was very negative."

"What? I thought they wanted to help Tanner."

"I guess not. They are more interested in covering their own asses, especially Thompson, who now happens to be sitting on the bench. They said if we call them it would waive the attorney-client privilege and we don't want to hear what they have to say."

"Well, what's that?"

Ted said with a laugh, "They refuse to tell us. They are asserting the 'privilege'.

Devin responded, "But the client can waive it, right?"

"I thought of that, but I think you should be the one to discuss it with Tanner now that you have finished with the Miao case."

Devin sat in the Vista jail attorney conference room with Tanner. He asked him what his trial lawyers could possibly say or do to derail their writ. Tanner responded that he could think of nothing, continuing, "I've told you everything that I told them."

"I need you to sign a waiver of the attorney-client privilege. I need to know what they will testify to in court before I decide to call them as witnesses."

Tanner was puzzled. "Why would they want to hurt me? I don't understand."

"I don't know. That's what I'm trying to find out," Devin replied. On his way back to LA, he called Brent who advised him that he was aware of the issue with the trial lawyers, but was otherwise ready. The evidentiary hearing was scheduled to start a week from Monday.

"Thanks for taking care of business, Brent. I've reserved a couple of two-bedroom suites at the Wyndham resort in Oceanside. Bring your family, if you'd like…one is yours."

Brent said, "Thanks a lot, Devin. I'm sure Connie would like that very much."

"Anything to make you more comfortable, my friend. It's going to be a totally new experience for me to be second chair as we work together again."

"Hey, it's always a treat to work with you. Remember the Pho Tang robbery case, otherwise known as the *Pun Tang* case?"

Devin chuckled, "Who could forget that? I still have a good laugh every time I think of it!"

Brent, with an embarrassed smile said, "Don't rub it in. See you next Sunday at the Wyndham. If you need me for anything before then, call. I've kept my plate clean."

Devin emailed Tanner's waivers to Knowles and Thompson, following up with a phone call. Their joint response was that they had not had him testify because he'd admitted to them that he intentionally put his hands down their pants, for sexual gratification.

Devin was stunned at their response. "Really? He flatly denies that. He has been adamant that there wasn't any sexual touching!"

Knowles said sharply, "Well, that's what we are going to testify to."

"That's totally inconsistent with what you have told me in the past. In fact, I have a recording of our conversation where you said as much."

Knowles shouted, "That's totally illegal!"

"So is lying under oath! You'd better think long and hard about what you're going to say because I'm calling you guys to the stand," he said calmly and hung up. Devin lied that he had recorded any conversations with Knowles, but on the other hand, Knowles had never told him that Tanner had admitted to any sexual touching. Devin believed Tanner was truthful, and it was consistent with what the boys had said.

The following Sunday evening, in preparation for the big court day on Monday, everyone met for dinner at a restaurant next to the Wyndham. After everyone was clear on their marching orders, they called it a night and went looking for a good night's sleep. Next morning a large group of friends and family, plus, a couple of news reporters, were waiting outside Judge Cole's courtroom.

Devin was really pissed off. "How in the hell did they know about the hearing?" He spoke to one of the reporters who told him that one of the family members told her about it. He was very concerned that the coverage of the hearing involving a convicted child molester trying to get a new trial would be big news. The reporters promised to report only the facts, no opinions. Besides, they knew Tanner's family. Devin didn't believe them, but at this point, he had no choice. He asked Beverly to find out who invited the news people and see what she could do to stifle any news articles. *Usually Devin liked his name in the press but this was an exception.*

The hearing started off in a very cordial manner; Judge Cole was a delight to be in front of. He gave each side a great deal of leeway in presenting their case. It was his decision that mattered in the end. Brent was very articulate and went through each witness with skill and precision, everything going as planned, no surprises from either side. The week went by quickly; each night they would gather for dinner and discuss the day's events. Devin was pleased and felt things were going their way.

The following Monday, it was Knowles and Thompson's turn to testify. When they got to court there was a commotion in front of Department C, with TV cameras and reporters in the hallway. Devin's stomach churned as he thought, 'what a terrible turn of events'. An attorney approached Devin and said that he represented NBC, and that he was going to ask the court for permission to set up cameras in the courtroom.

Devin remarked, "Over my dead body!" as the attorney walked away. So far, the print coverage had been fair and small. This was different – a total fiasco. The judge was up for re-election next year and if he decided on behalf of Tanner, the public would think he was soft on crime and had let a child molester off. That would surely put added pressure on him.

The whole morning was used up with arguments concerning the public's right to know and the defendant's right to a fair and impartial trial. In the end, Devin lost the argument. The judge allowed one TV camera in the courtroom to be set up in the back. However, it was a live feed to the public, like court TV. Brent played to the camera, his voice was quiet and direct, as he examined both the trial lawyers. They behaved. Devin thought they really believed that he had a recorded statement which would impeach their testimony. Interestingly, their recollections were very vague about advising Tanner of his right to testify and their reliance on the prosecution's honesty concerning Sloan's sudden disappearance from the case. They admitted they hadn't investigated it further. Tanner was their last witness, his testimony was guarded. Devin guessed that a few years in prison didn't help. The cross examination was aggressive; Tanner became defensive but he didn't break. Usually, if a person is telling the truth it comes out. Devin hoped the judge would see that.

Finally, the judge recessed for the day and advised the parties that he would provide his written decision within ten days. That evening Devin and Ted stayed up to watch the late news. It inserted a picture of Tanner as the commentator made editorial comments about the judicial system being unfair to victims of sexual assaults. Devin hoped that it would not influence the judge. Now all they could do was wait and see. On the eighth day, Devin received a telephone call from Beverly saying Tanner had been attacked in jail and had been transferred to a local hospital in serious condition. He was attacked by another inmate who had seen his picture on the TV newscast. He thought he was doing everyone a favor by trying to kill a child molester. Devin freaked out. A vigil was set up at the hospital.

The following day, Devin received the court's ruling, granting their writ which meant that Tanner was going to get a new trial. He called Beverly and the family members advising them of the good news. That evening Jerry Tanner died of his injuries. Devin was devastated. He closed his office and cried, yelling for the press to go fuck themselves! He wrote a blistering letter to the head of the news department for NBC saying that their biased reporting had just cost an innocent man his life and asked them to broadcast the true facts; that it was the court's opinion that Tanner did not get a fair trial and had granted him a new trial. That never happened. The news department failed... no, *declined*, to report it.

24

It took Devin a week after the funeral to recover from the tragedy. Ted and Ray were very supportive, knowing that sometimes Devin let his feelings get in the way. The day was gloomy and the pollution was brown and ragged as Devin sat, staring out the window of his office. Suddenly his cell phone rang. It was Jackson. He said, "Hey, boss. I have a new case. Attempted murder."

Devin replied, "I hope it's local. I'm tired of traveling."

"Guess what, boss? It's right here in Pasadena and the money is good. I spoke to Ray earlier in the week about the case and he told me to give you a couple of days off. He's already handled the bail, he's a pro. However, we all know you're the master."

Devin replied in a *'don't screw with me'* tone of voice. "Come on, Jackson. We've known each other too long for unnecessary praise."

"Okay, when can I bring the client in?"

"I want to talk to Ray first, so let's shoot for tomorrow?"

"How much do you need for the case?"

"Let me call you later about that," Devin replied and hung up. After Devin hung up he spoke to Ray advising him that he was on his way to the office to discuss the case referred by Jackson.

"Yes," Ray said. "Sounds like a great case for us, so I covered the bail through Kiperman. The arraignment date is in 20 days in Alhambra. Devin thanked him and asked Ray to fill him in. Afterwards, Devin called Jackson back and approved taking in the case, asking him to have his client come with him tomorrow and to bring $35,000 to cover the cost of the preliminary hearing.

"Done," Jackson replied.
The client's name was Benny Tsu. The information was kind of sketchy, it seemed that there was some kind of argument in a bar and the client, at some point, shot the victim. The bail was set at $350,000. *Nice payday for Kiperman.*

The meeting with the client was rather comical. His story went something like this: *He was at a local Chinese bar in El Monte with a couple of friends when he accidentally bumped into another patron, spilling his drink on the person. He described the person as a gangster type, a tall slender guy wearing a sharp looking suit. Visibly upset, he turned to Tsu and shouted, 'Do you know who you just spilled your drink on?' Tsu told him he was sorry but the person didn't accept the apology and he pushed Tsu away. As he started to walk away, the guy turned and said, 'I'm not finished with you!'* One of Tsu's friends tried to intercede, when this person pulled a gun on him. Security jumped in and kicked all of us out of the bar. We wound up in the parking lot and a crowd started to gather. Little did the guy know that Tsu also carried a gun. The guy said' let's take this around the back and finish it.' Tsu said, "Not on your life. I'll go only if you give up your gun". The guy handed the gun over to somebody in the crowd and then they both walked around the back, behind the bar and out of sight of the crowd. Tsu then confronted the bad guy, called him a punk as he pulled out his own gun, and shot the guy in the gut. The gunshot echoed, the guy fell to the ground, the crowd came running. Tsu dropped the gun on the ground, the police were called, the victim was taken to hospital, Tsu was arrested.

As it turns out, Tsu's a gangster in his own right. *Devin thought, this is not going to be easy.* There were a lot of witnesses, but no one actually saw the shooting. Tsu had refused to give the police any kind of statement, cLaiming to not speak English. The cops did not have a Mandarin interpreter. Devin asked Tsu, "Did anyone in the crowd know that you had a gun?" The answer was, no. At this point, Devin asked Tsu to wait in the conference room while he left with Jackson for a private conversation.

Devin was shaking his head, "Who is this guy?"

"He's a soldier for Liam Ho, who owns numerous clubs and massage parlors in the San Gabriel Valley. A very nice guy if you don't cross him."

"Do you know who the victim of the shooting is?" Mo said, no. "Can you find out?" Jackson replied, of course.

"Okay," Devin said, handing him an envelope containing $15,000. They both returned to the conference room where Tsu was waiting. Devin asked him if he knew the victim. He replied, no never saw him before.

"Let me ask you one more question about the gun. Is it registered to you?"

Tsu answered, "No, my boss gave it to me. I don't think that it's traceable."

"Okay, listen. Please don't discuss what happened with anyone. Just remember that loose lips sink ships." Tsu had no idea what Devin just said, but Jackson said something in Chinese of like nature. Tsu nodded his understanding. Devin told Mo to make sure he got him to the arraignment, *and to please remember that he was to only speak Mandarin!*

"Got it!" Mo said as he left. "I'll call you with the name of the victim."

Devin asked Ray to run Tsu's criminal history through their regular sources. An hour later he reported, he's clean. Three days later, Mo called

Devin with the name of the victim. "It's Sonny Peng, he's a regular at the Blue Penguin bar. The information I got is that he works for a casino in the City of Commerce."

"Thanks! I'll check him out."

As it turned out, he had a record of assaults with one conviction. It seemed that some of the victims of his assaults were reluctant to testify.
At the arraignment, Devin received the complaint and arrest reports, which included the names of numerous witnesses, although, no one had been witness to the actual shooting. Peng's gun, the one that was turned over to someone in the crowd, had its serial numbers filed off. It was the same type of gun allegedly used by Tsu.

By now, Peng had recovered from his gunshot wound but was still receiving physical therapy. The charge was attempted murder; Tsu plead not guilty. Devin had Mo hire a Chinese investigator to help with the digging because he was really interested in locating any witnesses who could support that Peng was the aggressor and, therefore, show his propensity for violence. He had no idea how he was going defend Tsu. It seemed that his conduct was deliberate and premeditated. He needed a self-defense theory - maybe it would come to him.

One evening while watching the movie, *The Matrix* on Netflix, it hit him. Keanu Reeves had two guns, he had emptied one and thrown it away and then pulled out another one and fired it. *What if Peng had another gun hidden on him so when he gave up the first one, he pulled out his second gun when they went behind the building? Tsu had grabbed for it, they fought for control and it went off, striking Peng.* Wow! that sounds reasonable.

The next day he ran the theory by Ted. "Where did that come from?" he asked, amazed.

"From a movie I saw last night!"

"You have a very creative mind, Devin, but how are you going to plant that idea in the client's mind so he can present the story to you?"

"I know, that's a problem. I guess I could give Jackson my theory on how the events unfolded and let him work with Tsu."

Since they didn't waive time for the preliminary hearing, it was the 10th day when they were in Judge Richard Montes' court. The prosecution presented a simple story based on the testimony of a couple of witnesses and Peng, as to what happened in the alley behind the bar.

Devin did not present his theory. However, he did establish that the two guns were the same make and both had serial numbers removed. The judge held Tsu to answer the charges and transferred the case to Pasadena for further proceedings. After court, Devin asked Jackson to meet him in the first-floor cafeteria with the client. He explained the need for getting their stories straight before returning to the court room. About 15 minutes later, the three of them were seated at a table in the back. Devin explained to Jackson that he needed to hear what happened, directly from the client's mouth. Jackson agreed and spoke in Mandarin with the client. About an hour later, it was a done deal. Tsu confirmed that Peng had pulled out a second gun; that he had struggled with Peng to get ahold of the gun, it discharged, striking Peng in the stomach. Devin now had his self-defense.

Two weeks later they were before Judge Bonnie Martin. Tsu plead not guilty. The DA offered to take the 'attempted murder' off the table, if Tsu would plead guilty to 'assault with a deadly weapon.' Devin knew that the offer was more than fair and, under normal circumstances, he would've forced the client to take it; three years beats fifteen, any day. He declined it.

The DA looked puzzled and said, "You know that's a gift, right?"

Devin replied, "I really do appreciate your proposal but I can't convince my client to take it. He wants his trial."

"Well, it's his funeral. The offer is withdrawn."

The trial was set off two months down the road, giving Devin plenty of time to prepare Tsu for his testimony. He had to be believable. If they lost, it would be 15 years in state prison.

25

Devin was relaxing in his office when Joel Carlton, one of his partners walked in and took a seat right in front of Devin's desk. He looked as white as a ghost. Devin knew Joel well and immediately knew something was seriously wrong.

"Joel, what's wrong? I can see it in your face!" He held his hand over his eyes, trying to swallow but his mouth was extremely dry. "I think I'm in a shit load of trouble, big trouble which will also affect our law firm. It's serious, Devin."

"Okay, just slow down, please take a deep breath and tell me what the problem is."

Joel started, "I represent Bryan Weeks, a client that owns and operates an import-export business; we've represented him for years. I believe him to be on the up and up. He primarily imports produce to the US from Mexico, South America, the Philippines and sometimes, from China. About three months ago, he flew me up to Seattle to meet one of his customers from the Philippines, who own a commercial fishing fleet and wants to market their catch in US. They wanted my advice on how to accomplish this, so I told them they would need a broker in the field to represent them in the US marketplace. I also told them our firm represents a food and produce broker with connections to numerous retail market chains, all over the United States. They asked if I could make the introduction, I told them, yes. About two weeks later, I had a meeting with Larry Elmont, who is president of Elmont International Produce, also a longtime client, to see if he was interested in brokering fish from the Philippines. He told me he could place the fish, but before committing, he would need to meet with the principles and get some samples of the product. I went ahead and arranged a meeting which took place in Portland, Oregon. They brought with them a case of fresh frozen fish and discussed quantity, prices and such and everything seemed to be in order. Elmont called me three days later and said it was a go, the samples of the fish checked out. I put the deal together and the firm received a big, fat fee. Well, last week the shit hit the fan! The ship that transported the fish from the Philippines arrived at the dock in Portland and, as planned, Elmont had his refrigerated trucks pick up the fish. However, for some godforsaken reason, the ship sank in the harbor. To keep the ship afloat and salvaged, the cargo had to be unloaded under the supervision of the Coast Guard. During the process, it was discovered that under the fresh frozen fish were tons of marijuana! The FBI and the DEA were called in. The captain and the crew were arrested, our client, Bryan Weeks, was arrested. The cops are now looking hard at me and Larry Elmont. I have been subpoenaed to appear in front of the Federal Grand Jury by the US Attorney's Office in Oregon. They said the value of the marijuana is over $4 million dollars! Now it's clear to me that the fish was a cover.

Joel looked ready to pass out. "Please help, Devin. I swear I had no knowledge of this and neither did Elmont. I feel awful that I got him involved, I'm sure were going to lose his business; worse yet, the DEA told me they had been looking at Weeks for the last few months. They believe he had been smuggling contraband into Miami for a long time with the help of an attorney there. This attorney, who also happens to be a high-ranking officer in the Coast Guard, is believed to have been giving Weeks information about shipping lanes so his smuggling operation would not be detected. Weeks is now cooperating with the Feds for a deal. He has given up the lawyer in Miami and told them that I was his West Coast attorney." Joel was shaking as he was speaking.

"Devin, I swear I'm totally innocent. Thank God it happened in Portland, where it's big news, and so far, we have been spared."

Devin sat there, his mind numb for a second. "That's one crazy story, Joel."

Joel winced, "I know, but it's all true!"

"Does Elmont have a lawyer yet?"

"I don't know. He's not communicating with me."

Devin's mind was spinning. "Who's in charge of the investigation?"

"John Moker of the FBI, and Justin Silver of the DEA. They're out of Portland, Oregon's office and the US Attorney is Nick Allen, also from Portland."

Devin asked, "Have you given anyone a statement?" Joel replied, no. "Okay, I'll take it from here. Who else knows about this around the office?"

"Not sure. I'm afraid that shit news travels fast."

"Well, let's get on top of this. We need to call a staff meeting right now and put a lid on this. We can't have this fish story stink up the place."

Joel said, with a weak smile, "That's not funny." Devin replied, sorry.

26

Devin, Ted and Ray spent the next few hours discussing the best way to approach the problem before it hit the local press; it could potentially destroy the law firm. The first thing to focus on was how to keep the word from spreading. They called each of the firm's employees into the conference room, one by one, to find out what each of them knew about the fish/drug connection. They quickly found out that only four people were aware that Carlton was in some kind of trouble. Fortunately, Joel was extremely embarrassed about the whole messy story and had kept it among himself, two of his secretaries and a couple of other partners.

Devin explained the necessity of keeping this information from leaking, in the interest of the firm's reputation and financial future. They all understood how rumors start and can grow like wildfire; the security of the firm was in their hands. They all knew they had to act fast.

Devin and Ted were in Portland late that afternoon. The plane ride was less than two hours, they'd barely had time to pack, unsure of how long this could take. They had scheduled a meeting with US Attorney Allen, Moker of the FBI and Silver the DEA investigator. When they arrived at the Federal Building in Portland, which housed the courthouse and the US attorney's office, they were greeted by Allen and given badges. They were escorted into a small conference room where Moker and Silver were seated. After brief introductions, Devin explained that he was the senior partner of the law firm where Carlton was a partner, and that he and Ted headed up the Criminal Defense Division. Explaining that the primary reason for their visit was the paramount concern of keeping any publicity about the case away from their firm, Devin told them the story from

Carlton's point of view. *He explained that Carlton was a straight-Laced conservative, deeply hurt that the finger is pointing in his direction. Devin assured them that he was willing to cooperate in any way needed, and that because of this incident, the firm had already lost one of its larger business clients, Elmont Produce. He explained that neither Carlton nor Elmont were aware of Weeks' background and/or his criminal activity.* Devin ended by asking simply, "How can we help?"

Silver replied, "Thanks for your willingness to meet and discuss our mutual interests. Our investigation has uncovered that Weeks had taken a couple of trips to the Philippines prior to our discovery. When we interviewed the boat captain and some of his crew members, they each gave a similar story stating that when the ship was loaded in the Philippines, Weeks and a person named Santos supervised the loading. The ship's captain came clean and told us he knew about the cargo but that his crew were totally unaware, that they didn't board the ship until after the containers were on board. None of them knew or had any knowledge about your partner, Carlton, or Elmont, but that doesn't mean they were not involved."

"As a courtesy to you, Mr. O'Neill, we will not jump to any conclusions. We have investigated the backgrounds of both your partner and Mr. Elmont and so far, they have both come up squeaky clean."

"I thank you for that," Devin said humbly.

Allen finally spoke up, "That doesn't get them out of the woods, however. Weeks is talking and pointing the finger at them both, as well as, some people in the Florida area. We've been advised that an investigation by the DEA office in Miami has been going on for a few months. We have Weeks on their radar and one of the things he's saying is that he gave Carlton over a hundred thousand dollars in cash, under the table, for his help in bringing in the marijuana."

Devin stayed calm, "What kind of proof do you have that it's true?"

Silver replied, "Nothing solid, yet. However, we have searched Weeks' residence in Malibu. Did you know he owns a couple of Ferraris worth around $1 million? We also found $750,000 in cash in a safe. He's a piece of work, but that's not our issue," he continued. "We have him cold. Our question is, how far does his criminal enterprise extend? We want to catch the bad guys."

Devin remarked, "Please, before you include my client, make damn sure you have the evidence, not just Weeks' mouth!"

Allen replied, "Of course. I would like to talk with Carlton about his finances, though. It would help. As I said, I'm not in the business of accusing or convicting innocent people."

Devin replied, "If I get him up here tomorrow, would that work for you?" Allen replied, yes.

Devin stood up and shook hands. "Okay. Ted and I will stay the night. What time tomorrow?"

"Can you make it around 11 am? I have a couple of short court appearances in the morning."

"That works," said Devin as he left the offices and called a cab. While on the way to the Marriott in downtown Portland, he called Joel and gave him a detailed description of his meeting with the US attorney and the investigators.

"Weeks is trying to throw you under the bus and told the investigators that he gave you $100,000 in cash for helping put the deal together." He paused, waiting for a response. There was silence on the phone.

"Joel, are you there?"

Finally, Joel replied, Yes, I'm here."

"What about the hundred thousand dollars? Is any of that true?"

Joel stuttered, "I can explain."

"Give it to me straight," Devin demanded, letting his growing agitation show.

"Yes, it's true. He gave me a hundred thousand in cash months ago. He said that he was buying a Ferrari and the seller wanted cash only. He asked me to hold it until he could raise the additional hundred thousand dollars. The car cost $200 grand, so I took his money and put it in my safe deposit box. About two weeks later, I gave it back to him so he could make his purchase."

"Were you present when he purchased the vehicle?" Joel replied, no.

"Where did you give him the money?"

"I met him at the bank, in the vault where the safe deposit boxes are."

"Did you have any other dealings with him since then?" Joel replied, no.

"Okay. Here's what I need you to do. Please bring with you a couple of years of tax returns and a recent financial statement and meet Ted and me at the Marriott in Portland. I'll text you the location. We have a meeting with the Feds at 11:00 tomorrow morning."

Devin continued, "Who else knows about the hundred thousand dollars? Joel said, no one.

"Keep it that way," he said, hanging up the phone with Joel and turned to Ted in the back seat of the cab. "Joel took the hundred thousand in cash from Weeks. His explanation sounds reasonable but what he did was stupid."

"What the hell?"

"I know, but he was only an escrow holder. Weeks was buying a Ferrari and the seller wanted cash. Joel says he only held the funds for a short time." Ted was incredulous.

"If that's traceable were all fucked!"

"Let me worry about that for now. Let's take a look at Joel's finances; based on my knowledge, I'm certain he's not a high-life kind of guy."

As they pulled into the Marriot, Devin said, "Let's check in, get some dinner and enjoy the rain. How does that sound?" The gentle rain was pouring steadily by now. It was Portland, after all.

At 9:30 the next morning, Devin and Ted met up with Joel in the Marriott coffee shop. They discussed the upcoming meeting over a light breakfast, while Devin looked at Joel's financials that he'd brought. They seemed to support Devin's opinion that he was a fiscal conservative; his net worth was approximately $2 million, consisting of real estate, which included his home valued at $750,000. By LA standards, that was modest. His stock portfolio, retirement accounts, personal property and vehicles covered the rest. His salary and profit participation in the law firm was about $300,000. His credit rating was in the top 5%, so there was no reason for Carlton to indulge in criminal activity.

Devin took a sip of his coffee and tried to put Joel at ease. "I know that being in your position is very uncomfortable, but from my experience, I believe we can put this to bed, today. First, I'm going to let you answer all their questions. I can't see you being tripped up. So, please listen carefully and only answer the questions asked. If I think there is need for an explanation, let me handle it, okay? Don't be nervous and get all sweaty." He laughed lightly, trying to put Joel at ease. "Are you ready to rumble?" Joel let out a nervous laugh and said, yes.

They arrived promptly at 11:00 at the Federal Building. They were quickly escorted into a large conference room where Allen was seated. He rose from his seat and greeted Devin, nodding to Ted and Joel. Moker and Silver remained seated at the table, along with a court reporter.

Allen started the proceedings immediately. "Mr. O'Neill, I took the liberty of having this meeting recorded and reported. I hope you don't mind?"

Devin was caught off guard, but tried to not overreact. "I would have liked a heads up, but I have no objection."

Allen continued, "I also have to give your client the admonishment. I prepared a document for your client for that purpose, asking him to read and sign it," he said as he handed the pleading to Devin.

After reading it thoroughly, Devin handed it to Joel, giving him the okay to sign it. With all that concluded, Devin informed them that his client had brought his financials as requested. "I have copies for your review only. You may make a copy, but they are for your eyes only as it concerns this investigation."

Allen had his secretary come in to make a copy of all the documents provided. Soon after, the questions were flying from Silver, Moker and Allen. Joel handled himself like a pro. About two hours later, they took a recess for lunch. After the lunch break, Allen thanked Joel for his candor. Answering all questions directly, the only exception was when he was asked about the hundred thousand dollars. Joel denied any knowledge of that, as instructed by Devin.

In concluding the meeting, Allen said, "We have discussed your responses. We find them credible and unless some evidence points to the contrary, we are going to consider the matter closed. You will still have to testify before the grand jury and at Weeks' trial, if the case goes that far. And you will have to waive the attorney-client privilege. Are there any questions?"

Devin was trying not to breathe a visible sigh of relief as he responded, "That works. However, if Weeks' attorneys assert the privilege, we will have to abide by the court's ruling. I just wanted everyone to be clear on that?" Allen replied, of course.

At that point, they all rose from the table and shook hands. As Devin, Ted and Joel left, it was a little after 3:00. Joel was all smiles and some of the color had returned to his face, finally.

"Devin, I can't thank you enough! I thought I was a goner for sure!"

They returned to the hotel and immediately went to the bar. Joel downed a couple of glasses of Scotch, neat. Devin had a glass of wine and Ted, a glass of water. He had been clean and sober for as long as he could remember.

Devin called Michelle during the taxi ride to the hotel, asking her to book their return flights to LA. The best she could get was a 10 pm flight, arriving back in LA after midnight.

27

During Devin's first meeting with the US Attorney he was given the name of Larry Elmont's attorney. Devin knew Robert Phelps, so during the wait for the return flight, Devin called Phelps. Their conversation lasted over an hour and when it was concluded, Phelps had a completely different take from his original point of view. Devin proposed a meeting with himself, Joel, Phelps and his client. Phelps agreed, hoping to also get his client out from under the cloud. Additionally, Devin hoped to restore Elmont's business for Joel.

The following Tuesday they all met in Phelps' Wilshire office. Elmont apologized to Joel for thinking the worst; they both were now on the same page and greatly relieved. But until Weeks is convicted, they pledged to be government witnesses, with the knowledge that they might have to face accusations by Weeks' attorneys in a public trial.

Between his meeting with Phelps and Joel Carlton's pending testimony before the grand jury, Devin tried hard to stay focused on the work needed for the next case up for trial, the Benny Tsu case. Ray and Jackson had been working on the client, hoping to drill the events of his story into his head until he believed *(remembered)* that this was how the events happened. Devin had decided to have a practice run through with Tsu, playing the role of the prosecutor. During his questioning, he used Jackson as a translator *(because he only spoke Mandarin)*. At the conclusion of the role-playing, he gave Jackson a wink of approval. They were ready. Ray had prepared the case for trial, and all Devin needed to do was show up and do what he did best.

On the day of trial, Judge Martin advised both, the DA, Phil Cohen and Devin, that she was currently in trial. She gave them the choice of starting the trial with her on the following Monday, or she would send the case to the master calendar court, to be reassigned to another judge. Devin, not knowing who that new judge might be, opted to wait the week. He advised the judge that on that Monday, he had to assist one of one of the attorneys from his office, who was testifying before the Federal Grand Jury in Portland, Oregon. It was agreed to have a two- day delay, starting the trial on Wednesday. Whew!

The following Monday, while Devin was seated in the hallway waiting for Carlton in the Federal Court building in Portland, he received a panicked phone call from Jackson, saying they couldn't find Tsu. Apparently, he had taken a trip to Las Vegas over the weekend and hadn't returned. Devin tried to calm him and remarked, "Well, here's the deal. We've already been paid, so don't panic. We'll worry on Wednesday if he's a no-show, right? What's the worst that can happen?"

Mo replied, "I know that's the last thing you need to hear, boss. Sorry to bother you."

When Devin returned from Portland the following day, they still didn't know Tsu's whereabouts. Ray was pissed off, but stated that they weren't his babysitters. "It's not Jackson's fault if he's a no-show, but you know Mo. He will blame himself if he thinks he let you down.

Devin replied, "I know."

The morning of the trial, Ray picked Devin up at his home and they drove to the Pasadena courthouse. Devin's mind was not totally on Tsu. He was thinking about Carlton's testimony, and even though it had been just what the US Attorney had ordered, he was still concerned about the potential future of the law firm. Ray noticed that Devin seemed distracted and asked if he was all right?

"Yeah, fine. Let's just hope Tsu shows up today." When they arrived at the courthouse there was a long line wrapped around the corner, waiting to go through security. Devin and Ray walked to the front of the line (*a lawyer's perk*) when they saw Jackson waving his hands to get their attention, he pointed thumbs down. Devin looked at Ray as they walked past him and said, see you upstairs... we can talk then. They disappeared into the building, taking the elevator to the fifth floor, to Judge Martin's courtroom. As they entered, Devin saw Philip Cohen seated at the prosecutor's table. He greeted Devin and Ray with a smile and a handshake. Chuckling, he said, "I guess you are here for your client's funeral, right?"

"Could be, Could be." As they started to settle in, the clerk advised them both that a jury panel would be up by 9:30. At that moment, Paul Hon, the court interpreter walked into the courtroom. Devin knew him well from previous cases he'd handled. He was easy to work with. Devin went to greet him and asked him to stick around. Ten minutes later, Jackson arrived and they quickly adjourned into the attorney conference room, located just inside the courtroom. Trying to appear calm, Devin asked, "Where is Tsu?"

"I spoke with him last night and we planned to meet in front of the courthouse this morning. He never showed up. I made some calls while standing in line, one of his friends told me that he was arrested last night in Las Vegas! Nobody knows for sure what happened, but he is being held by ICE at the North Las Vegas jail. That's all I know."

Suddenly, the bailiff knocked on the door and said, "The court is ready for you. A jury panel of 35 are in the hallway, waiting".

Devin had to think quickly as he entered the courtroom. The judge was already seated at the bench. She said hello to Devin, but before he could reply, she said, "When the clerk finishes with a jury panel, we can start." She started to get up to go to her chambers and Devin interrupted and said, "Your Honor, my client is not here yet. I need about 15 minutes to find out where he is?"

She looked at her watch, "His excuse better be a good one or I'll remand him during the trial. Then we'll be sure he'll be on time." Devin replied, thank you, and returned to the conference room. Ray was already on the phone with Chris Kiperman, the bail bondsman, telling him it was an emergency. Could he locate Tsu, whom they believed was in the North Las Vegas jail?

There was a long ten minutes of silence before Chris called back, saying that their man was being held on a Federal warrant by ICE, for some kind of immigration scheme; providing false documents of some kind. "He's due in Federal Court in Las Vegas sometime today. Anything I can do to help you guys?"

Ray was shaken by the news and all he could say was, "Thanks, Chris. I'll get back to you."

He shrugged his shoulders and told Devin, who told Jackson what Chris had said.

"What now, boss?" Jackson was crestfallen.

"I'll inform the court of what we've just learned. There will obviously be no trial today. I'm sure the court will issue a bench warrant for his arrest." Jackson suggested they should just get him out of jail in Las Vegas.

Devin replied that it would be very expensive, that all they could do now was get information about his arrest. Jackson replied, "Now that I know what's going on I'll see what I can come up with."

"No need to stick around, go make your calls," Devin responded as he entered the courtroom and advised the judge why Tsu was absent. Needless to say, she was not happy. She issued a no-bail bench warrant and excused the jurors, who couldn't have been happier.

On the drive back to the office, Devin said to Ray, "I didn't like the case from the very beginning. It's not my style to create evidence to win a case. I had second thoughts about putting on our defense because it was *our* defense, not the client's. So maybe God was telling me something."

28

Once back in the office, Devin learned that Weeks and others had been indicted. *What a day, Lordy, what a day!*

As he walked back to his office, he saw Nancy Young seated in the waiting room. Michelle alerted him of her presence, telling him that she had just shown up and refused to leave until she could meet with him. She was well known around the office ever since Devin had gotten an acquittal for her husband on a manslaughter charge. She was one of the few grateful clients that would do anything and everything to help promote Devin's legal career. Devin got to his desk and buzzed Michelle, asking what she wanted to speak to him about that was so urgent? Michelle informed him that her son, Eric, was just arrested and charged with murder. That's all she knew about it. Devin went out and greeted her and invited her back to his office. She had tears in her eyes as she walked, her mouth trembling. Devin took her by the hand and told her everything would be all right, even though he knew nothing about the case. When they reached his office, he asked her to sit on the couch, as he pulled up a chair. She put the briefcase on the coffee table in front of her, and before any conversation took place, she opened it up and removed a folder containing numerous newspaper clippings. He asked her if she would like something to drink. She said no, Michelle had taken good care of her while she waited. She handed him the clippings and said, please read.

As he looked through the clippings, one headline read, *"Gang murder in Suburbia*. As he read down the article, it said *'Inner cities no longer have the exclusive on gang violence. It's come to rural Ventura. A young mother, while holding her four-month-old baby was shot and killed by a bullet that went through the front window of her parent's home in a middle-class neighborhood, fired by local gang members of the Ventura Street Gang. Witnesses told police that shots were being fired from a white Chevy Tahoe as it drove by a group of rival gangsters who were gathered next to a public park. Bullets went flying in both directions as the car sped away. On one side of the park were single-family residences, one where the victim and her baby lived with her family.*

Another article referred to the Sheriff's investigation of the shooting. They had they located the Chevy Tahoe, registered to Eric Young, who was later arrested along with three other alleged gang members. He read other articles which covered the DA and Sheriff's press conferences where they informed the public of the arrests made of those individuals who'd been charged with the murder of Cindy Taylor, the young mother. Fortunately, the young child was unharmed. The articles did not disclose any names of the charged individuals or details of the crime.

Devin put down the papers and looked at her and said, "I'm so sorry." She replied that he had nothing to do with it.

"What do you mean?"

She wiped her tears and blew her nose and unfolded her story for Devin. *At the time his father was being prosecuted, my son was just starting high school. Unfortunately, all my focus was on my husband's situation. He got into a bad crowd and became a member of the Ventura Street Gang. To this day he still has a gang tattoo. I knew I'd lost control of him during this time. He had been stopped by the police on numerous occasions, for really nothing, but he was already identified by the cops as a gangster. By the time he was a senior in school, his grades were so poor and his attendance so sketchy, that he was not going to graduate. When his father was acquitted, thanks to you, his father took control. Eric listened to him for the first time in a couple of years. He turned his life around, but his gang affiliation did not go away. He claimed them as his friends, sometimes his best friends. We realized we needed a change of scenery, so we rented out our house in Ventura and moved to San Diego. We enrolled him in a private school as a senior, and with the help of tutoring and his teachers, he successfully completed school. He changed friends, he was a completely different person. We were proud parents, again. After high school, he attended San Diego State for two years then he decided he wanted to become a Marine like his dad, so he joined. We moved back to Ventura. Three weeks ago, he came home on leave from a one year assignment in Afghanistan. When he went to San Diego State we helped him buy a Chevy Tahoe. When he enlisted, we kept it at our home for when he returned. He is now 22 years old. Some of his old friends found out that he was back in the neighborhood and they started coming around our house; they had not changed, they were no good. However, they seemed to kind of look up to Eric since he was now a Marine. He was polite to them but kept his distance. About two weeks ago, one of his old gang buddies, Danny Stevens, asked if he could borrow his Tahoe, he had to move some furniture from his parent's house. Eric gave him the keys and he returned the vehicle the next day. The day after that, the police were at our door. They seized the truck, had a search warrant for our house; they searched Eric's room and claimed to have found gang materials and pictures of Eric in the old days, with his fellow gang members throwing gang signs.*

Her calm manner dissolved and she was in tears again, searching her purse for a Kleenex... *They took him into custody, his dad told him not to say one word, no matter what, and ask for* a lawyer. *I thought they would let him go, but they didn't, and now they have charged him with killing that poor young girl. He wasn't even there. They didn't care, they claim his car was used in the shooting. They found a couple of empty cartridges under the seat.*

"Devin, he is innocent! You saved us once, please, can you help us again?"

"When did this happen?" *She replied, last week, Wednesday.*

"Where was Eric at that time?" *He was home, he didn't go anywhere. Remember, he lent his car to Danny Stevens, who, by the way, was also arrested, along with a couple of other old acquaintances.*

"Did he have a cell phone? Yes."

"Do you know if he made any calls from it that evening?" *I don't know, but the police seized it from his room.*

"Has he been to court yet?" *No, he's due to go tomorrow.*

Devin said, "Okay, I'll make some calls and cover the court appearance. Bail is going to be set very high based upon the charges, so he'll have to stay in jail for the time being. The case is going to get heavy press, so it's imperative that we counter it as much as possible. I'll call for a press conference of our own and present our position. It's not going to be a level playing field, but it will help. I'm going to hire the same investigator that I used for your husband's case, Ed Ruddy. I guess the question is, how are you going to pay for all this, Nancy? Are you guys able to do this?"

She replied, "We own our house free and clear and in today's market, its worth over $1 million. I can write you a check right now for $30,000. It's everything we have in the bank, Devin, but my husband is good with this."

Devin responded, "Make it $20,000. I expect the fees and costs could be in the range of $150,000 to $200,000 depending on where the case goes. We'll worry about that next.

Nancy replied, "I'm not worried. You have always been very fair with us. We trust you completely."

"Thank you. Hold on for a moment..." He called Ray into the office and introduced him to her, since they'd never met. Devin gave Ray a brief rundown and asked him to contact the DA and the court and advise them that we were going to be representing Eric Young. Nancy wrote out a check for $20,000 and handed it to Devin.

He gave her a big hug and said, "I'll see you tomorrow in court, Nancy.

29

The drive to the courthouse in Ventura could take a couple of hours from LA, depending on traffic, unless you knew all the shortcuts. *It was going to be a long day on a slow treadmill.* Ray had reported back to Devin that the DA handling the case was Ken Riley.

"That's great," Devin replied. "I know him very well. He's a really good guy. I have tried many cases with him. I think I'll give him a call."

Riley got on the phone and said in a friendly voice, "Devin, how are you? It's been a while."

"I've been keeping pretty busy. By the way, I still can't thank you enough for your efforts on that child molestation case. I understand that you're handling the Eric Young matter."

"Yes, I am He is charged along with three other defendants, all charged with murder. It's a terrible tragedy, a young mother shot in the head while holding her baby. The community is enraged, the press won't let it go; they are partially blaming the police for not protecting the community from the local criminal gangs that have been terrorizing our neighborhoods. It's a hot one. Will I see you at the arraignment?" Devin replied, "Yes."

"Well, get up there early. There's going to be a crowd of demonstrators at the courthouse, they're yelling for blood; they want the death penalty."

"Who's handling the arraignment?"

"Judge Steel. He's presiding. He's allowing TV cameras in. Not my idea. It's going to be very high profile, so wear your best suit," he said with a chuckle.

"I always do, for the cameras."

Riley continued, "All the other counsel are local, you're the only out-of-towner."

"I'm not looking forward to seeing good ol' Judge Steel. As I recall, we didn't get along well on my last case before him."

Devin arrived at the Justice Center off Victoria at about 8 am, and there was already a huge crowd in front of the courthouse, maybe a hundred or so carrying signs - *Kill the bastards! I support the death penalty, and a few more, less mentionable.* Devin had to walk through them to get to the front door and through security. Fortunately, one no one knew who he was now, but by the end of the day, he would be a household name in Ventura. He cleared security, went directly up to the second floor and down the hallway to the DA's office. Once at the window, he asked for Riley. The girl behind the window said, 'He's already in court, Department 36, third floor.' *(She sounded like an old-fashioned elevator operator.)* Devin rode the elevator up one floor and when the door opened, there was a crowd in front of

Department 36, TV reporters, camera equipment lining the hallway, and a least five deputy sheriffs standing around. He worked his way to the front door and approached the sheriff who was in full tactical gear.

Devin said, "Good morning! I'm one of the defense attorneys, Ken Riley is expecting me. Can I go in?" The sheriff gave him a slow once-over look and asked, "What's your name? *Devin O'Neill*. He disappeared inside, returning in 30 seconds giving him the go-ahead.

The courtroom was empty except for TV camera people setting up. Devin approached Ken, who was with two other attorneys. Ken introduced Devin to Roger Dodd, a Public Defender, and John Regis, from the alternate Public Defender's office. Ken explained they were waiting for Lloyd Smiley, who would privately represent Danny Stevens.

"When we're all here, the Judge wants to see us in chambers. He wants to avoid a circus, so he wants pre-arranged dates for the prelim. I assume that you're all going to want to waive time?" he asked as he handed Devin the *murder book,* containing over 100 pages, plus 2 CDs and 3 DVDs in the package.

Smiley arrived shortly, sweating and taking short gasps. Because he was a well-known, local attorney they had to sneak him through the back door so he could avoid the growing mob which was getting hostile. *Introductions all around, again. Devin knew him from before. Not sure from where...*

The clerk took them all back into the Judge's chambers, the meeting was very cordial. The judge was familiar with all the attorneys, commenting to Devin that it had been a while since their last encounter.

Devin replied, "Your Honor, it's nice to see that you haven't changed a bit." The Judge laughed and immediately eased the tension.

"O'Neill, You're a hell of a lawyer. I'd even consider calling you if I ever needed one myself!" Everyone laughed, Devin thanked him, and they quickly got down to the business at hand.

Judge Steel began, "First, concerning bail, I'm going to go with the bail schedule. It calls for two million, including enhancements. I've been informed that the DA is not seeking the death penalty. Even though this crime is disgusting, we're not going to mention that, one way or another, in open court. I also expect you will want to continue the arraignment or set a date for prelim setting, with appropriate time waivers? I will grant it, you'll need to discuss this among yourselves."

Smiley said, "I think we can all agree on a preliminary setting date somewhere between 30 to

45 days out? This should give us time to review the voluminous discovery." The clerk pulled out the court's calendar, declaring there was a date open in 60 days. All agreed.

The judge continued, "I'm allowing the victim's relatives into the courtroom and any of your client's families, if they wish to attend. I've set aside a row for the press and any seats left open will be for the general public. I will excuse you now. Go talk with your clients, they are in the courtroom lockup. Please let my bailiff know when you are ready, but I admonish you to make it short and sweet. See you in the courtroom, gentleman."

Twenty minutes later the arraignment was over and the defendants were returned to the lockup. Devin had gotten Eric's mother and father into the courtroom to watch the proceedings. There had not been an empty seat to be had. Devin and the three other attorneys waited in the courtroom to allow the crowd to disperse. The sheriffs all did their job well and the crowd left quietly, without incident.

Prior to the arraignment, Devin met with Eric for the first time, in the lockup. Eric was a good-looking kid, about 6 feet tall with an athletic build, a short Marine haircut. He was outfitted in jail orange, chained around the waist and ankles. He was very polite as Devin explained the rules, responding, yes sir.

"We're going to let things cool down a bit, Eric. I've had a talk with your mom. I know you're not involved and I'm confident that you will be exonerated. I know the DA personally, and he's a very fair man. Right now, he must push hard to keep a lid on everything to prevent the community from exploding. So, I'm advising you to keep your mouth shut. I'll be up to see you in a couple of days after my review of the evidence. Bail has been set at two million, so at the present time, you're not going anywhere. And listen carefully, when you're in court it's important to stand up straight, as there will be TV cameras covering your every move. All you need to say is 'Yes, Sir' to a couple of questions. I'll be right next to you. Do you understand all instructions?" *Yes, sir.*

After the arraignment, while the lawyers were waiting for the court to clear, they exchanged business cards and agreed to meet in a week or so to discuss the case, without trashing each other's client. As Devin was leaving the courtroom, he was confronted by TV reporters with the cameras going right in his face. Devin who had been there many times before, identified himself as Eric Young's attorney. He told the reporters that he could not comment on the evidence but was confident of his client's innocence and that once he had read the reports, he would be happy to answer their questions. He handed out approximately 20 business cards and received the reporters' cards in return. As he walked down the hallway to the elevator, he yelled back at the group make sure you spell my name correctly... two 'l's. With a laugh and a small wave, he entered the elevator.

Once outside the courthouse he walked with Nancy and her husband, Ron, to their car, chatting for a few minutes. He suggested they keep a low profile for a while, explaining that he would be speaking with them soon. Back at the office he had Michelle make copies of the *murder book* for both Ted and Ray. The local evening news carried the story under the headline 'Criminal Gangs Terrorize Ventura County causing the death of a young mother.' *He was always amazed to see himself in front of the cameras, looking cool, collected and professional. Amazing!*

He knew things would die down for now, but would definitely heat up again at the next hearing. The following day he received a telephone call from

Eric's mom, thanking him for all he was doing and explained that they were working on getting the money together. Their broker had told them the loan should go through within a couple of weeks. In the meantime, they were going to take a short trip to San Diego for a few days to get away from all the nasty stares.

"Good idea! I'll be up to see Eric in a couple of days. We're working through the discovery."

30

It took three days to digest all the reports, photographs, evidence seized, statements of witnesses, etc. They made their notes, evaluated the evidence and formed opinions on how to defend the case. At 8:30 in the morning, Devin, Ted, Ray and Ed Ruddy sat around the conference table, Eric Young's file was spread all over the table. Michelle had brought in coffee and doughnuts for them, they were ready to roll. Devin started the meeting by asking Ted for his slant on the evidence, based on the police reports and all they'd reviewed.

"Well, the first thing we have to do is distance our client from the event. The reports put his vehicle at the scene, by a number of witnesses; one of them actually wrote down the license plate number. Others took pictures with their cell phones, and one provided a video of the aftermath of the shooting. Nothing that I saw identified any of the occupants in the vehicle, but it's clear from what I saw that there were four people in the Tahoe; two were wearing baseball type caps, they were seated in the driver's and front passenger seat. That's about all you could see. The police identified the gang bangers in the park from some photos. They were 19 Street Oxnard, a Hispanic gang. Unfortunately, the interviews of the gang members turned up nothing. They denied being at the scene at all, even though two of them were clearly identified from the photos, they still denied seeing or knowing anyone in the white Tahoe. The defendants were all identified from fingerprints taken from the interior of the vehicle, including our client's. Obviously, our client's fingerprints can be easily explained. It was his vehicle and you would expect to find his, but not the others. At this point, their prints are not my major concern.

He continued, "Two spent shell casings were discovered on the floor in the back seat of the Tahoe. They matched the caliber of the bullet that struck the victim. During the search of two of the defendants' houses, three guns were found but they were not the murder weapon. That's still not been recovered. The search warrants included our client's residence and some of the items seized from his room were some old photos, taken at least 4 to 5 years ago, with some members of the Ventura Street Gang. They were showing off their gang tattoos and throwing gang signs, but nothing recent was found. Unfortunately, all four defendants, including our client, still have gang tattoos.

The report by the gang expert stated that he was very familiar with Ventura Street and their rivals, 19th Street Oxnard. This was not the first time they had fired on each other. They have an ongoing dispute from way back, ever since one of the gang members in Oxnard was killed by the Ventura Street Gang. He also identified Eric as a current gang member, based upon field ID cards and some prior arrests. Further, he states Eric's gang moniker is slick.

Devin knew that if you looked beyond his 'obvious' findings, the expert couldn't really rely on the field identification cards or anything else that he'd come up with, to establish that Eric is a current gang member. Especially given the fact that his last contact with him was over four years ago. The good news was that, thus far, none of the other defendants had said a word. A real plus!

Devin asked, "As you know, the police took Eric's cell phone. Did they seize any of the other boy's cell phones?"

Ted said, "Yes, but they haven't yet been analyzed, that I'm aware of."

"It's my understanding that the phone company can trace the whereabouts of those phones at the time of the shooting, which could place some or all of the defendants at the scene, right?"

"Yes, that's accurate. Also, if any of them made calls, depending on whom they called and what they said, could incriminate them." Devin asked Ted if he found any additional information that could be used against Eric. Ted replied, no.

Devin then asked Ray if he had anything to add. He responded, yes. "The problem, as I see it, is that even if Eric was not there; if somehow it can be proved that he gave the Tahoe to Stevens, knowing that he was going to use it in a drive-by against 19th Street Oxnard. That would make him as guilty as the others. In my opinion, we need to show that Eric had disassociated himself from the gang, since moving back from San Diego.

Ray shifted gears, "I wonder if there are any communications between Eric and the others that could show that he was out of the gang? Anything in writing or otherwise, to show that would be good. We need to interview his friends, his teachers in the SD area, possibly including his activities and assignments while in the Marines? We should also take a hard look at the Prosecutor's gang expert, Allen Carrington. We need to impeach his credibility, if we can, because he's going to say Eric is still a gang member, even though he'd been away for a while. He will assert that his proof is that at the time of the shooting, he was still hanging out with his old gang buddies and he either drove the Tahoe or lent it to the others, to go to war with Oxnard."

Devin agreed. "You hit the nail on the head, Ray! I'm going to assume that his cell phone never left his house that evening, nor did he. Even so, as you say, he could have lent the car to the others with full knowledge of their plans."

He turned to Ed, "I'm going to turn the ball over to you. I think a good place to start is to find any evidence to discredit their expert's opinion. Hopefully there's something there. Eric's family will be very helpful in pointing you in the direction of witnesses who have been in contact with him since living in San Diego; we need to show a life change. In the meantime, guys, I'll be going to see the client this afternoon. I hope to get as much background information from him as I can, that would help you. Be thorough... I believe in his innocence." As the meeting broke up, Michelle came in and handed Ed a copy of the complete file and a check for $10,000.

31

That afternoon Devin drove up to the Ventura County jail, located adjacent to the Justice Center. He had called in advance to secure a conference room for his interview but they didn't want to give it to him. He called Riley immediately and explained that he was getting the cold shoulder. "No worries, it'll be handled." He arrived at the jail at 2 pm, sharp, being mindful of the time allotted for his interview. When he entered the jail, he got cold stares from the jail personnel; they did not like that he went over their heads, but they complied with Riley's request.

Devin sat in an all-glass private room in the attorney conference room. The deputies there were keeping a close eye on him. He waited for over a half hour before they brought Eric in, chained at the ankles and his wrists were chained to his waist. He had to shuffle to move, they sat him down. Devin asked them to please remove the chains around his wrists. They denied his request, so he made a stink about it. The sergeant in charge responded and complied. Devin knew he was in hostile territory and concerned about his conversation being listened to and possibly recorded. He told Eric to be careful, to only answer the questions that he asked.

Eric replied, "I understand. Thank you for representing me."

"You don't need to thank me. I believe in your innocence." At that point, he started asking questions about his friends that he'd made in San Diego; his teachers, his tutors, if he had any jobs, the names of his employers and any Marine personnel who knew him, his commanders and superiors and anyone who would be able to testify as to his character. What was his specialty in the Marines and what was his assignment during his tour of duty?

They discussed why he kept his tattoos, what did his gang moniker mean and how did he end his involvement in the gang? Why did he continue to keep gang photos in his room? Did he make any calls from his cell phone that evening? If so, to whom and why? Why did he involve himself with some of the gang members when he came home on leave? And finally, why did he lend his vehicle to Stevens?

Devin made notes of each and every answer. Eric was articulate and polite, his responses were direct and to the point. *He answered that when he enlisted in the Marines the question came up about his tattoos and any gang affiliations that he might have. He told the recruiting sergeant all about his prior life before moving to San Diego. He believes that all that information is contained in his Marine file. He was asked to show some proof that he had left his gang life behind, so he wrote letters to the gang members that he had addresses for, advising them he no longer considered himself to be a gang member and that he was moving on and going to join the*

Marines. He sent those letters out and gave a copy of each to the Sgt. which he also believes are in his Marine file.

That information was exactly what Devin was looking for. He would give all this to Ed to follow up on. When he left the jail, he drove down highway 101 back to LA. As he pulled out of the parking lot, he noticed an unmarked sheriff's car following him. He was followed all the way to the LA County line. He drove very carefully as not wanting to give them any opportunity to pull him over. *He smiled to himself. Do I look that naïve?*

32

The following day, he gave Ed his notes from the interview with Eric. He also called Riley and reported the surveillance incident.

Riley replied, "Sorry about that. Let's leave it alone for now. I'll make a note of it and I'll notify the court."

Devin was really pissed off about how he was being treated by the Ventura County Sheriff's Department, so he wrote a letter to the court with a copy to the head Sheriff. Taking his own advice about sitting on things like that for a while before acting on them, he re-read it and decided to shelve it. He scolded himself for reacting on his emotions. *Breathe…*

A couple of days later he found himself sitting in Lloyd Smiley's office, along with the other defense lawyers. Everyone was spinning the facts to minimize their client's guilt, but they all eventually agreed that none of their clients would testify nor implicate the others.

Devin's position was that his client would testify only to the following: *That he was a Marine on leave, that he had removed himself from gang banging years ago, that he had lent his Tahoe to Stevens the day before the shootout and that he had no idea or knowledge, about any shooting or what had happened.* He further agreed to share his investigator's reports, if they reciprocated. Devin then told them about the behavior of the Sheriff's Department toward him. At first, they thought it was funny and then they had a different take on it. *Wait! Why would the cops be afraid of O'Neill? Was there a hole in their case?*

33

Three days later, Devin received a call from the US Attorney in Portland, advising him that Weeks had pled guilty and was sentenced to seven years; that to get that sweetheart deal, he'd had to testify in Miami against his former attorney and the Coast Guard captain, who had been a part of the conspiracy to smuggle cocaine from Columbia into the Miami area. He thanked him for the update.

Devin still felt a level of concern. Even though Carlton's matter had ended gracefully, he knew that one simple mistake by any of his partners or staff, could affect the future of the law firm and his standing in the legal community. He thought about discussing the matter with his partners. He was assessing the potential impact on his life...he had just turned 58, his youngest child was now a Junior at the University of Arizona; maybe it was time to retire from the firm. He rolled his chair around and gazed out the window... his favorite way to consider all options.

After giving it more thought, he decided it was best to sit on the problem for a while and let some of the dust settle. If he was in the same frame of mind later, then he would talk with them.

How does one spell – conundrum?

As fate would have it, he received a call from Ken Riley who said, "My boss has directed me to take the case to the grand jury for an indictment and bypass the preliminary hearing. The grand jury is going to convene a week from next Monday. I've just advised your co-counsels."

Devin asked, "Why? Your case against most of the defendants is really strong! Did the cops screw something up, or what? So, tell me, who's afraid of us cross examining your witnesses? This is bizarre!"

Riley replied, "No one, to my knowledge. It's a decision made by the higher ups. That's all I know."

"When do you think the indictment will come down?"

"I'm not sure, but I will notify all of you and advise you of the arraignment date as soon as I know."

"Where is the case going to be assigned?"

Ken said, "Department 42, before Judge William Celli."

"You mean Wild Bill Celli? Tell me you're kidding, right?"

"Yep! One and the same...Wild Bill Celli!"

Devin couldn't believe his bad luck. "You're killing me, Ken."

"Not so. Listen, just because he carries a gun under his robe doesn't make him favor our side more than yours."

"Sure, it does! What did Smiley think when you told him? Ken replied, he just laughed.

"You know, I could file a 170.6 motion and remove him from the case."

"That would only make matters worse. Don't do that, Devin. Trust me!"

"Okay, I do trust you. I just don't want to get screwed with no reaction."

Ken said, "He was a colonel in the Marines, a war hero. He's your best bet."

"Well, thanks for the heads up, Ken. Are you staying on the case?"

"Yeah, as far as I know. And by the way, I expect to win and then get that promised appointment to the bench!"

Devin laughed, "I'll vote for you!" as the phone went dead.

34

Devin called Ted into his office and gave him the news. Ted commented that this would move the case forward faster and they'd lose their ability to cross examine the People's witnesses. "We better advise Ed that now we are on a short leash, don't you think?"

"I don't think it's going to affect us as much as the other defendants, but we have drawn a tough judge, Bill Celli."

"Yes, but he's fair and won't be swayed by community sentiment."

"Okay, I trust your judgment. I've never been before him, only heard of his reputation."

Devin called Nancy to explain the new development. She became hysterical, "What are they trying to do to my boy?"

"Calm down, Nancy! Nothing has changed except we will be in court a lot sooner. Don't worry, we are totally in control. I will need some more money from you soon, though. Can you bring in $25,000 within the next few days? We are now on a fast-track."

She pulled herself together. "I can do better than that. Our loan was approved and we're signing the documents tomorrow. We'll be getting the money the following day and I'll bring the hundred thousand dollars."

Devin said, thank you.

35

There was a lull at the office, except for a little excitement surrounding the settlement of a civil case, in which the firm represented an adult film company.

Sunset Films, who made and marketed hard-core adult movies, had sued one of its producers over the rights to the name, Seymore Butts *(see more butts, really?)* The victory came after a lengthy trial that caught the eye of the public. When it was over, Devin congratulated Jeff, one of the law partners, on a great job. Joseph and Rita, the owners of Sunset Films, threw a party for the law firm, which included the actors and actresses and others who participated in their movies. Invited guests included the judge and members of the jury; they all showed up except the judge. It was a bizarre event, to say the least, but a good time was had by all! The door swag (gift) that everyone received was a box of Seymore Butts *(see more butts)* movies. The party favors and delicious treats had to be seen to be believed. *A great relief that no media had been invited...*

The day after the party, a grand jury convened. Devin, Ted and Ray met with Ed who had previously prepared and distributed a preliminary report of his investigation before the meeting. The information was positive. *Ed had interviewed many witnesses from Eric's San Diego days, including his friends, teachers and his tutors, who all had good things to say. Most of them said that Eric had told them about his past gang life in Ventura; they quoted him as saying, "that life was in the past." Two of his employers also spoke highly of him and his work ethic. His report cards for his senior year in high school and two years at San Diego State, averaged B+ or better. Marine Sgt. Kimball, who recruited Eric, said that they freely discussed Eric's reasons for wanting to become a Marine and his future goals, and further, that he was proud that Eric had become a Marine. He had a recruitment file on Eric which he claimed included letters and other evidence of Eric's disclaimer of being in a gang.*

He had also made clear that he could not release the file, that it would have to be subpoenaed; but he assured Ed that it would be helpful.

Ed concluded his report with, "I have not spoken to his commander at Camp Pendleton or his commander in the field, but as is it was explained to me by the recruiting sergeant, he was in an elite special squad which few qualified for. Only his commander is authorized to divulge that information."

Devin was thrilled with all he'd heard. "I guess his Commanders will need to testify. And that's a good thing, since our judge was a colonel in the Marines. I'm sure they will have Eric's back." He thanked Ed for being so thorough, then moved on to the rest of his research.

"Okay, your report indicated you have information about the Prosecution's gang expert?"

Ed looked at his paperwork, "When I tell you what I found, you will understand why they wanted to avoid him testifying at Eric's preliminary hearing."

"Well, don't keep me in suspense. Let's hear it!"

Ed said, "Here goes... *Three years ago, he was employed as a police officer by the City of Oxnard. He was suspended from the force by the Police Chief for lying under oath about how he handled two related drug cases, and for falsifying his testimony and evidence to convict an alleged gang member.*"

"Wow! How do I prove that?"

"Easy! He was brought before the Police Commission where the evidence was presented. It's all in the transcript of the hearing."

"Was he ever prosecuted for perjury?"

"The answer to that is, no. The DA just dismissed the cases; they didn't want to open up a Pandora's box."

"How the hell did he get hired by the Ventura County Sheriff's Department?"

Ed said, "As a member of the police union, his attorney had friends in the Sheriff's Department, so I guess they overlooked his indiscretions."

"I wonder if Riley knows about this? How do we get our hands on that transcript without showing our hand?"

"Leave that up to me. You will have it soon."

Devin's mind was going a mile a minute. "I hope it includes the names and case numbers of those involved. What do you know?"

"It definitely will! They were all local Ventura cases that have to be recorded."

Devin smiled and said, "Nice work, Ed. I'm sure the schmuck testified before the grand jury, telling them that Eric was a gang member. Please follow up on the Marines and get me the Commanders' names and, hopefully, the

Recruiting Sergeant will be able to get you his enlistment file? Once Eric has been arraigned, I'll file a discovery motion to get his cell phone inspected for all calls and their locations on the day of the shooting. Do you have an expert who can perform those tasks?"

Ed replied "Yes, no problem." They all stood up and high-fived.

When Ed left the conference room, Devin said to Ted, "I'll try to find out if Riley is aware of his gang expert's background? What do you think?"

"I think you should leave the whole thing alone. It's a bad idea to make any inquiries right now. If he knows that we know, all he has to do is find another expert without any baggage." *Right as usual.*

Ted added, "I guess it's doubly important that we get our hands on that transcript, without anyone being the wiser." *Devin called Michelle in and asked her to cut Ed a check for $10,000.*

That evening Devin felt like celebrating, he took his wife, Ted, Ray and his girlfriend, to dinner at Mastro's, in the heart of Beverly Hills. They shared a bottle of expensive champagne - except for Ted, who had iced tea.

36

Devin's drive to Ventura to attend Eric's arraignment was uneventful, until he reached the Ventura County line. Within a few minutes, he noticed a Ventura County Sheriff's vehicle a couple of car lengths behind him. It followed him all the way to the Victoria exit. Devin pretended not to notice, but it was clear in his mind they were trying to intimidate him. *Sorry, It's not going to work...*

He met with all the other defense counsel in front of Department 42 to discuss how they wanted to handle the arraignment. It was agreed that since all their clients were in custody, they would enter pleas of 'not guilty' and force the case to trial, within the statutory period of 60 days. This would not only put a burden on them to be ready, but it would also put a scare on the prosecution because it's rather unheard of not to 'waive time' in these types of cases.

Devin kept from the other defense counsel the information his investigator had discovered. He figured when he had all his ducks in a row, then and only then, would he share with the other attorneys.

When Devin and the others entered the courtroom, he was shocked to see TV cameras being set up with numerous reporters milling around. He saw Ken talking with the clerk. Devin approached him and asked what was up with all the news coverage?

Ken replied, "It's not my idea. My office is playing this for the community and the Judge seems to be going along with it."

Devin and the other attorneys requested time from the clerk for a brief chambers' conference before the proceedings. He left and went into chambers. Returning after a brief visit to the judge, he announced that the judge would see them. The judge's chambers were filled with numerous pictures of the Judge with political leaders, including the President of the United States. There was also Marine memorabilia everywhere.

The Judge stood as they entered. He was in his late 60's. He stood erect in his six-two frame, sporting a short military style haircut, his piercing blue eyes looking directly at them. He held out his hand and shook each attorney's hand, saying, "Gentlemen, it's a pleasure! What can I do for you this morning?"

Devin immediately introduced himself as Eric Young's attorney and exhorted, "Your Honor, my client objects to the unnecessary publicity that will be created by the news media. Being allowed to broadcast the arraignment is going to impact getting an impartial jury and potentially, a fair trial.

The Judge responded, "Mr. O'Neill, I understand your position, but I've been overruled at this point. The local press filed a brief requesting public access to the proceedings and I agreed, with the limitation that they may not photograph the faces of any of the defendants, for what that's worth."

All the other attorneys also voiced their objections. The judge said "Sorry, gentlemen. They're going to stay. You don't have to talk with them. Mr. Riley is not a champion of the press either but, his boss," (he said with a laugh,) "is running for re-election next year and he's the one pulling the strings."

Devin was impressed by the demeanor of Judge Celli. The arraignment took 10 minutes, not guiltys were entered when it came to set a pretrial, and trial date. Riley's mouth fell open when the defendants unanimously refused to waive time. The Judge, at that point, set a pretrial date of 45 days out, with the jury trial 15 days later. The bail remained the same $2 million each. Before they concluded, Devin filed his formal discovery motion for the inspection of Eric's cell phone. The court ordered that the inspection would only take place at the sheriff's department. The order included Devin's expert having access to the phone there.

When Devin left the courthouse, there was a small crowd outside who booed him as he walked through them into the parking lot. He was being chased by reporters with microphones pointed at him, yelling questions. Devin ignored them. They even came up to his car and tried to block him from backing out of his parking space. Somehow, he did so without running anybody over. That night the local stations in Ventura ran a feature story about the arraignment and the attempts to get Devin to speak with them. Fortunately, this was not big news in LA, so it was hardly reported.

Again, Devin was escorted to the county line on his way back. Devin laughed to himself, thinking, *you're not going to see me again for 45 days, so I hope you have something better to do than follow me*.

Devin told his partners that he would be involved in preparing the Young case for the next 45 days. Ted would be the 'go to' guy, concerning all other criminal cases during this period. He did not waste any time, starting the day after the arraignment. With Ray's help, he started to accumulate a list of witnesses, evaluating each one, reviewing the items evidence that they intended to introduce. Ed was the key link feeding them information daily. The report on Carrington's firing from the Oxnard PD was on Ray's desk. It contained the names of the defendants and the case numbers involved. Ray was at the Ventura County courthouse, in the clerk's office making copies of each of those files. Listed, also, were the names of the defense attorneys. *This was the start of Carrington's demise.*

Devin called each attorney on the list who had conveyed the sordid details on how Carrington lied, planted evidence, and falsified arrest reports. This had caused the cases to be dismissed, eventually. In fact, one of the defendants who was wrongfully convicted and incarcerated, filed a civil rights lawsuit against the City of

Oxnard and the Police Department, and it was settled almost immediately, under seal, so that information was unavailable. The witness list kept growing. They added Max Vigil, the Chief of Police, the three police officers of the review board and the Oxnard police officer who reported Carrington's conduct to the Chief. They now had the transcript of the hearing and all the court files of each case that was overturned, due to Carrington's perjury.

    Devin directed that all this must be kept under wraps until the time was right. Ed's expert, Phil Richards, inspected Eric's phone and was able to pull off phone calls made on the day of the shooting. To accomplish this, he used the assistance of the phone company to track the location of the cell phone throughout that day and night. *Eric had made four outgoing calls that day to persons in the San Diego area; he also received six incoming calls from the same area.* The cell tower tracking proved that the phone did not leave the Young's residents that evening. Subpoenas were prepared for the phone records, including the cell tower tracing from Verizon and Phil Richards. However, all this, *still* did not prove that Eric was not at the scene of the shooting. It helped a lot, but Devin still wanted the information from the Marine Corps. *This could hit the bull's eye!*

37

Devin drove to Oceanside at the request of Ed and Sgt. Kimble. They had set up a meeting with the Base Commander at Camp Pendleton. Devin brought a subpoena for the Commander and the Recruiting Sgt. which included access to Eric's files. Devin had to serve a subpoena before the Commander would agree to a face-to-face. Devin drove through the main gate and was directed to Command Headquarters. He didn't realize how big the base was. It took a good 20 minutes to find his way around, before finally entering the parking lot. He had to go through security where the sentry guard called him in and directed him to a parking space. He felt like he was in another world. In the lobby, Ed was waiting for him. Ed explained that they wanted to hear from his lips the facts that proved Eric was innocent. They didn't want to be part of defending a guilty person, even if he was a Marine. Devin commented he thought that a little unusual.

Ed remarked, "The military have their own rules, they want to be impartial."

A few minutes later, they were escorted into Commander Sharp's office. It was befitting a president; walnut paneled walls, the Marine Corps emblem was behind his desk, with the seal of the United States very visible. Devin was a little surprised that Commander Sharp's rank was that of a General. He introduced himself and Sgt. Kimble, who was already in the room. He looked the part; he stood rigid at 6'1"with a short Marine haircut, steel gray eyes. He gave Devin a broad smile as he shook his hand. He was wearing fatigues as if he were going to war, but his demeanor was far from it.

They all sat around the conference table and he asked for the subpoenas. Devin produced them and handed them to Ed, who served them on the general and Sgt. Kimble.

He glanced at them quickly and said, "Now that that's out of the way, what's the story about one of my soldiers?"

Devin went through the evidence for and against Eric. Devin concluded that there was no question in his mind that he was innocent of the charges.

Sharp asked, "So what do you need from the Corps?"

"I need verification that he had withdrawn from gang life when he entered the Corps. It's my understanding his file contains such proof."

Sharp replied, "It's our policy that we don't take gang members into the Corps, and although I don't know your client personally, Sgt. Kimble has all the confidence in him. I've looked at his record in the field and found that he's one hell of a soldier. We will produce the records as you request, however, we need assurance from the judge that they will be used for that limited purpose."

Devin replied, "Our judge is Bill Celli, retired Marine Colonel. I've been told he's a war hero, so I don't see any concerns there."

After they left the building, Devin had Ed sign off on the proofs of service. Over the next couple of weeks, Devin outlined his opening statement, met with Ray to discuss and prepare the jury instructions, and prepared written Voir Dire questions, which hopefully the judge would allow, concerning any pre-trial publicity which could potentially impact the seating of an impartial jury. They carefully drafted a pre-trial motion covering a change of venue. *Devin was getting comfortable with Judge Celli.*

The pre-trial hearing was upon them. They were ready. At this point, Devin had not discussed anything with the other attorneys, except for their review of the grand jury testimony which included Carrington's testimony. *The trap was set.*

38

Devin telephoned each of the defense lawyers. He knew it was time to bring them on board about the Carrington information. It was agreed by all to meet at Lloyd Smiley's office, after the pre-trial hearing. All Devin had told them was that his investigator had uncovered some very damaging information about some of the prosecution's witnesses. They were anxious to hear it.

That Wednesday, Devin and Ray drove to Ventura for the pre-trial hearing. Ray was blown away that they had a police escort from the Ventura County line to the courthouse. "You are one popular guy, my friend," he said.

Devin smiled and said, "Yes, I know."

Judge Celli had set aside the entire morning to discuss the case. Because of its notoriety, the courtroom was, again, packed with press and spectators. Celli, realizing that the community's eyes were upon him, told his clerk that when all the attorneys arrived, they and their clients were all to be seated at their respective counsel tables. The clerk stood at the doors and instructed the attorneys about the Judge's request.

Once they were all in position, Judge Celli came out of his chambers and the bailiff called court into session. Judge Celli looked around the filled-to-capacity courtroom and asked each lawyer to announce their appearance and indicate the presence of their clients.

When that was accomplished, Judge Celli stood up and said to the attorneys, much to the chagrin of the gallery, "Gentleman, shall we all retire to my chambers?" Each attorney was asked to waive their clients' presence. They all agreed and quickly disappeared through the back door of the courtroom into the judge's chambers. The Judge took off his robe and said to the confused attorneys, "Gentlemen, relax. I'm not interested in mob rule here, so we can all speak freely. I want this trial to run smoothly and I need your candid input to make that happen."

The first question he asked was, "Is there any chance of this case being settled?"

Riley responded, "I can only offer them a plea to the charge and leave the sentence totally up to the court."

"That's not what I wanted to hear, but I do understand your plight. How long do you project this trial to take?" Opinions varied from three weeks to two months.

The judge said, "I'll set aside two months but let's hope it doesn't go beyond that."

Devin broached the issue of jury selection, saying that process, alone, could take 2 to 3 weeks. "The pre-trial publicity is going to make it very difficult to find an impartial jury, Your Honor."

"I completely understand, so I've decided to start with a jury panel of 350. I'm going to ask each of you to submit written questions for the panel. You can do this individually or in a group, but please submit them at least

10 days prior to trial. I will set a date five days prior to the trial, to review the questions. On the first day of trial, I will distribute the court-approved questions, then recess for three days, during which time we can address any motions you may have. After the jury panel returns with their written answers, you'll have 24 hours to review the responses, then I will listen to any motions for cause. I would hope that by the end of that process, we will still have 100 or so potential jurors to go through the regular process." All counsel agreed.

Judge Celli finished his directions, "I want witness and exhibit lists filed and exchanged, at least 15 days before we start the trial." Devin was impressed by the thoroughness and evenhandedness of Judge Celli.

Then he threw out a bombshell, "I have a motion on my desk from a documentary news production company wanting to film the proceedings. They're doing a documentary on criminal street gangs in the suburbs and have requested to set up one out-of-view camera during the entire proceedings. They will commit to not airing the documentary until after the completion of our trial, including any verdicts and/or sentencing. I wanted you to know that I'm considering their request."

At that point, all defense counsel voiced strong objections. Devin said, "No way! Not until hell freezes over!"

Judge Celli responded, "I would expect nothing different from you, Mr. O'Neill. All I said was, I was considering it. Nothing more. I'll let you know more after I've had the opportunity to analyze their request."

He stood up, concluding the meeting with, "Well, Gentlemen, I think we've covered it all unless anyone has something to add? If not, let's go back to the courtroom, put this on the record and face the crowd."

Twenty minutes later, the trial date was set for 45 days out. The crowd dispersed, slowly looking at all the lawyers. Devin, Ray and the others arrived at Smiley's office approximately 30 minutes later. Smiley's office was in old town Ventura, up from the old courthouse. It had a great view overlooking the Pacific Ocean. It was a well-appointed office, complete with wood paneled walls and plush carpeting; his plaques and awards very evident. They were escorted into a conference room which looked like an old school law library, the shelves all covered with law books. On the back wall, was a granite counter with plates and glasses and a variety of sandwiches, coffee, water and soft drinks. *Lloyd was a gracious host.*

After getting their food and drink, they took seats at the conference table and Devin, in his usual style, started the meeting. He spoke for almost an hour while the others listened and ate their lunch. They were incredulous about some of the stuff they learned about Carrington's past legal history. They all agreed that it was great stuff to have and use against him, and they considered all options of how to present it to their advantage. But even with all they'd learned, they were still not sure how much it was going to help their clients.

Devin responded, "You're wrong! Remember that there's no visual identification of *any* of the occupants in the vehicle. The prosecution needs to put your clients in the Tahoe, as gang members, in a shootout with Oxnard! They are relying 100 percent on their gang expert, so if his credibility falls, it really helps all of you."

Devin continued explaining the fact that his client had to testify about why his vehicle was at the crime scene. "It will be up to Stevens, who had borrowed the vehicle, to explain what he did with the Tahoe. I need to disassociate Eric from his vehicle at the crime scene because that's an undisputed fact that connects him to it. At this time, the prosecution does not know that Stevens had possession of the Tahoe that night. The big question is, how do you deal with that?"

They all looked to Smiley, hoping for a logical explanation on how he could testify without implicating the others.

Devin lowered his voice, "I'm sorry I have to do this. I don't want to hurt anybody else's case, but I've got my client to protect. I suggest that Stevens *not* testify and take the fall. I think if he testifies, he could bring all your clients down with him." The consensus in the room was that he should *not* testify. The question was left open for them to ponder. *(A conundrum?)*

Devin and Ray exited the meeting, leaving them to figure the solutions that best served their needs. *It was rush-hour traffic... of course, it took three hours to get back to Beverly Hills.*

39

Devin did not want to get involved with any other cases. Forty days would come up fast. He asked Ted to carry the load until Eric Young's case was over. He kept in touch with Smiley to see where they were concerning the Stevens issue. He knew it would be Smiley's decision in the end. Smiley had suggested to Devin that if Eric didn't testify, the prosecution couldn't possibly put any of the defendants in the car.

Devin replied, "Well, yes, I agree. But the fact is, it's my client's Tahoe that the shots were fired from, the casings were found in it, and my clients' fingerprints were also in the car, along with those of some of the other boys. How would you handle that?"

Smiley remarked, "I know. I know. That's a problem. Everyone's trying to come up with another solution."

"Yeah, I've looked at this from every angle... I can't think of one. We can't say the Tahoe was stolen because it wasn't reported stolen; and even if we claimed that, how do we explain that it was back in my client's possession the following day? Everyone would see through that immediately. The only logical answer is that Eric had to have lent the Tahoe to somebody he knew. I don't see another way out, but I'm all ears if anyone has a better solution. Otherwise, Stevens should take the fall.

A few days later, Devin and all other counsel received a minute order from Judge Celli approving the documentary production company's access to the trial, on the condition that the film and/or video tape would be sequestered until the end of the case. He left open the right to file objections, which he would hear prior to jury selection. Devin was not pleased, but he'd have to live with it.

Time went by quickly. Devin met with Eric and his parents three times during this period. He would have ample time to prep Eric after the trial began, since his case would start at the end of Riley's presentation, which would go two to three weeks into the trial. Ray was responsible for making sure all the witnesses, including experts and impeachment witnesses, were kept informed about their on-call status.

Devin decided to stay in Ventura once the trial started. He knew that driving back and forth every day would take its toll on his nerves and he wanted to be fresh and on top of everything. It was time to present the questions for the jury. Devin sent 312 questions to the judge for his consideration; each of the lawyers presented their own set of questions.

After reviewing the submitted stack, the judge was not happy. There was too much duplication so he ordered them to consolidate their lists into one. It took the better part of the afternoon to compile a joint list. 280 questions were re-submitted for his review. He explained that he'd select the most appropriate ones and any objections could be put on the record.

On the first day of trial, 350 questionnaires were handed to the jury panel with instructions to complete within the next three days. That gave the lawyers time to argue various issues, including the filming of the trial. Judge Celli listened patiently to each attorney's position before making his rulings on the record. *Some won and some lost.*

The jury responses were given to each attorney for review. Devin took one look at the volume of answers and immediately objected to the judge that they only had 24 hours to review.

The judge remarked, "Sorry about that. Maybe you should've asked fewer questions? You all agreed to the timetable and I'm sticking to it. You better get reading."

Devin and Ray returned to the hotel and divided up the list. They separated the list into *ACCEPTABLE* and

UNACCEPTABLE piles, and, although they knew what they were looking for, they weren't finished until after 10 that evening. They weren't happy that the *UNACCEPTABLE* list kept growing, leaving only 57 good ones. It was clear there was a bias against the defense and they should be excused. *Devin hoped the judge would see it his way.*

The following morning, each lawyer had their list ready for the judge. The judge took total control over the process, going through one juror at a time, attorneys making their objections and when they were finally done, Judge Celli had excused 231 of the 350, for cause. The remaining jurors were back in court at 1:30; the trial hadn't even started and Devin was already tired. He bitched to Ray at lunch that this pre-trial stuff was torture. By Thursday, he hoped they would have a panel by the end of Friday so they could get started in earnest. He didn't like living in a hotel but was grateful it wasn't a death penalty case, otherwise, he could be there forever.

The jury questioning went on and on, but they were done around 4 o'clock Friday and were excused by the Judge, who admonished everyone to be back at 9 o'clock sharp, Monday. *Hallelujah!*

Devin almost ran to the car, calling his wife to warn her about a week's worth of his dirty laundry. The weekend brought him back to life, a movie and dinner with friends, took his mind off the trial for a while. Monday morning his tunnel vision would be back, and always in the back of his mind, was the concern about what the other attorneys could do to screw up a good case. He needed to just unwind...

They decided to drive up separately in case Devin needed Ray to take some road trips. Everyone was on time, including the jurors. The Judge was happy for that and thanked them all as he prepared to seat a panel of 12 with 4 alternates. They were excused until 1:30 to finalize some issues regarding the production company's assigned location. The issue as to where the camera was to be located was dealt with by Judge Celli, who decided it would not face the jury. *No intimidation needed in his courtroom.*

At 1:30 everyone took their place. Eric had permission from the judge to wear his Marine dress blues and he looked sharp, the other defendants cleaned up nicely, too. It was time for opening statements and Ken Riley was performing. Devin knew he was a good lawyer and he lived up to that, speaking clearly while using photographs and diagrams to explain his case. He held the jury's interest. He addressed each defendant as a gang member, promising to prove so through the testimony of his gang expert, Officer Carrington. He explained that Carrington, who was familiar with Ventura Street Gang and other area gangs, would connect the dots leading to this terrible tragedy that had resulted from their gang activities.

Devin was eating it up. The more Riley was spouting off about Carrington's knowledge and expertise, the more stunned he still was at the ignorance of the DA's office regarding his past. Riley was finished in less than an hour and the defenses took their turn making opening statements. Devin had previously discussed what he thought each defense counsel should do. He recommended that if they had a tight alibi for their client, they should make an opening statement; if not, they should reserve it. Smiley was first to go, he reserved. One by one all the others reserved. Devin was last, he also reserved.

The judge was surprised by this. Usually, the defense wants the jury to know what their client's stories are, upfront. He figured they had some sort of cohesive plan... Celli asked Riley to call his first witness and he called the parents of the victim. They were followed by the coroner who testified about the cause of death. Then came the eyewitnesses, followed by the investigating police officers, whose job it was to lay out the crime scene; the search and seizure of the Tahoe vehicle and other items taken from each of the defendants' residences. The attorneys cross-examined each defendant only to establish that no one had seen their clients at the scene of the shooting. All the videos and photos taken by cell phones could only establish the license plate number of the Tahoe. Since none of the defendants had made any kind of statement, the prosecution's primary target was Eric. To get there, Riley needed Carrington to prove, by circumstantial evidence, that this was a gang shooting and all the defendants were in the gang. At the end of the week, Riley advised the judge that he only had one more witness and that was Officer Carrington. The judge excused the jury until Monday. After they left, he asked that when Riley was finished, the defense should discuss in what order they would like to present their case. Devin was still uncertain about Stevens and he would again discuss that with Smiley, but he figured he should go first because he knew Eric was going to place Smiley's client in the Tahoe. *Decision made.*

40

Today was finally Devin's time for show and tell... his time to shine. He and Ray drove to Ventura with their usual Sheriff's escort, laughing smugly. Immediately at the start, Ken Riley had his gang expert on the witness stand. He was taking him through his expertise, his training and his field experiences with various street gangs in the Ventura area. Devin was impressed by the way he handled himself and played to the jury. The questioning continued all morning, the jury listened and the camera in the back was rolling, taking all this in.

Just before the lunch break, Carrington started to testify about the rivalry between the Ventura Street Gang and the Oxnard gangs, explaining it was very violent. He shook his head, saying he couldn't even count the number of shooting incidents that occurred over the years, which eventually led to the death of a couple of Oxnard boys and the serious injuring of some Ventura Street members.

Devin's ears were like bat radar. He was anticipating the explanation of his role in these activities when he was with the Oxnard Police Department. But, he never brought that up. He inferred by his testimony that he had always been a Ventura County Sheriff in charge of the gang enforcement detail, and left it at that.

After the lunch break he was back up on the witness stand, identifying many Ventura Street Gang members who had previously been convicted of various crimes involving attempted murder, robberies and assaults, auto thefts. His goal was to establish that the Ventura Street Gang was a criminal enterprise. He then proceeded to identify each of the defendants as current gang members, showing pictures of each one with their gang tattoos, and pictures of them throwing gang signs. He identified each one's gang moniker. He claimed to know each one personally, by contact in the streets, explaining that during those contacts, he wrote what are called, field identity cards. He claimed to have numerous ones on each of the defendants.

When Riley asked him specifically about Eric Young, he stated that he was known as one of the ring leaders, although, he had not seen him around for a couple years, until recently, while investigating this case. He loudly volunteered, *once a gang banger always a gang banger!*

He continued by giving his opinion about the shooting that took the life of the young lady in this case, saying it was typical gang activity when confronting a rival gang. In this case, however, an innocent person had been caught in the middle. He acknowledged that he was not the investigator assigned to the case, but he was proud to have put his share of gangsters behind bars

Devin was lying in wait, keeping his objections to a minimum, letting the jury know that he was there and paying attention. Otherwise, he was happy to let Carrington ramble on. By three in the afternoon, the dog and pony show was over.

Judge Celli addressed the lawyers, "We can start your cross examination after the afternoon recess. Who's going first?"

Devin rose from his seat and responded, "I guess I'm the chosen one, Your Honor." This made the jury laugh. Twenty minutes later, Carrington was back in the witness box. Devin was standing and slowly walking back and forth, as the jury's eyes followed him, stopping directly behind Riley. He looked directly into Carrington's eyes, and in an even-toned voice said, "Good afternoon, Officer Carrington. Do you recall taking the oath to tell the truth this morning?" *Carrington replied, yes.* "I hope you live up to your word, sir." *Riley objected.* "Why would you object? Do you think he's going to lie?"

The Judge immediately jumped in and said, "Cut it out, both of you! Please behave like lawyers." *Devin apologized to the court.* "Officer Carrington, you were fired as a police officer by the Oxnard Police Department for lying under oath, weren't you?" *Before he could* *answer, the next question was, "*You falsified police reports and have given perjured testimony in court to send innocent people to prison, haven't you? *Riley was on his feet yelling objection, objection!*

The judge said, "I want to see both of you right now at the bench!" Devin, Riley and the others huddled at the bench. "Mr. O'Neill what kind of game are you playing here?"

Devin responded, "It's not a game, Your Honor. I have a list of impeachment witnesses and supporting exhibits," he said, handing over a folder. "This guy is a liar and a fraud and I can prove it! My questions are legitimate and, depending on his answers, I'm ready to prove that he falsified police reports, testified falsely to get convictions, and that he was turned in by his fellow officers. Shall I go on?"

The judge said, "Stop, please. Before I take up this matter, I'm going to excuse the jury until tomorrow." They returned to their seats as the Judge excused the jury, leaving them full of unanswered questions. He also excused Carrington, admonishing him to return the following morning.

Devin was on a roll. He knew that everything had been filmed by the documentary film company... sweet revenge. When they all went into chambers with the court reporter, the judge wanted everything that was said on the record.

Devin said, "I wish to make an offer of proof, Your Honor."

Celli said, "Go ahead, this should be interesting."

"First, here is my witness list and my exhibits to back up what I'm about to tell you. Carrington, for whatever reason, while in the Oxnard Police Department decided to be judge, jury and executioner. He intentionally falsified numerous police reports, then submitted them to the DA's office for criminal filings. Turns out, this occurred more often, than not. His fellow officers finally got tired of it and turned him in to the Chief of Police. Also, in two unrelated gang shootings, he identified two innocent young men as gang members, claiming they participated in the crime. None of them were gang members or participated in any criminal conduct. Because of his testimony, the DA filed charges against them. Carrington gave perjured testimony; they both got convicted and were sentenced to prison. To make matters worse for himself, Carrington tried to get his firing overturned, so he went before the Police Commission. Here's the transcript of that hearing." He pulled out the report and handed it to Celli.

"He even lied before *that* board, digging a deeper hole for himself. They upheld his firing. If you read the transcript, the evidence of his guilt is overwhelming. Interestingly, his attorney at that time, was none other than the brother-in-law of the Ventura County Sheriff. And guess what?" he continued. "Three months later, Carrington was hired by the Ventura County Sheriff's

Department; a political favor? I don't know, but they turned a blind eye to his past conduct which, in my mind, would have prevented him from even getting a job as a dogcatcher!"

Devin paused for effect and said, "But, wait! I'm not finished yet. Your illustrious DA, quietly, under the table, dismissed all the charges against those defendants that I've been talking about. But he *never* filed perjury charge against Carrington. I can only guess at the reason, Your Honor. If this became public, how many cases would this affect? Maybe hundreds of convictions could be overturned, a black eye for the DA and law enforcement. So, they covered it up!"

"One of the two young men who went to prison sued. His case was immediately settled under seal, so no one involved could disclose anything about it."

Devin said finally, "I feel bad for Ken. I'm sure he knew nothing about this. He's one smart lawyer and if he had known, Carrington would be nowhere near the courthouse. He knew we would be looking into the backgrounds of his witnesses."

Judge Celli sat there and listened until Devin was finished. He didn't say anything for a few minutes, just sat and remained silent.

Devin looked at Riley and said, "I'm sorry."

The Judge finally said, "Mr. Riley, you know your whole case has just blown up in your face, right? I must allow Mr. O'Neill to go forward, so I think you should ask your boss to get his ass down here right now! I think from my tone, you know I'm really pissed off." Riley left the chambers without saying a word.

Smiley was quietly applauding Devin from his seat. He knew the consequences for the DA and the Sheriff, if this case proceeded any further. There would be an investigation, the DA would be lucky to keep his law license, and he could kiss any of his political aspirations goodbye. As for the Sheriff, his hiring of such a criminally-minded misfit, would surely cost him his job. They had put the judge in a position where he would have to report what he'd just heard.

Devin looked at his watch, it was 4:30. They were still waiting for Riley's return with his boss, *waiting for the proverbial shoe to drop.*

The judge excused the court reporter and about ten minutes Later the DA showed up.

"I understand you want to see me?" he asked.

Judge Celli almost came out of his shoes, yelling "You're fucking damn right! I have a good mind to put you and your fucking Sheriff friend in handcuffs right now! You have both fucked up this highly visible, critical murder case! Sit down, dammit! I'm going to allow Mr. O'Neill to introduce everything he has. Ironically, this should bury you, after you were so instrumental in getting the documentary film company to cover the trial. I expect when they air their film, you better find a big enough rock to hide under. What a travesty!"

It was 5:30 when the judge told him get out of his chambers. The judge told everyone else, "I'll see you tomorrow at 9:30, unless you hear something to the contrary." He walked away, totally spent.

Everyone filed out quietly. Smiley said to Devin, "Can I buy you a drink? Shitty as this was to hear, you just saved all our clients' asses. I think the DA has no choice but to dismiss, and since jeopardy has attached, it's over."

Devin was exhausted, but happy. He said, "No, thanks. I'm done for today." He and Ray returned to the Piermont Hotel where they'd been staying, and went directly to the bar. Devin kept looking over his shoulder until Ray asked, "What's up? What are you doing?"

"I expect to see the Sheriff at any moment." Ray said, you're paranoid. *Maybe, but that does explain the daily escort.*

Tuesday morning Devin arrived in front of the Judge Celli's courtroom. It was still locked. The other lawyers were congregated at the end of the hall, he didn't see Riley or Carrington. Finally, the door opened and the bailiff told the jury to wait outside. When Devin entered, he did not see the cameras or anyone from the documentary film company. They were usually there, setting up early. Riley entered the courtroom through the back door. Devin had guessed he'd been talking with the judge.

Riley came over to Devin and said, "It's over. I've filed dismissals, with prejudice, against the defendants. I think they're all guilty, not sure about your client. Also, I want you to know I just resigned from the DA's office. This is more than I can stomach."

Devin replied, "I'm really sorry. That's a life-changing decision, but I respect you for that. I hope one day you get your wish and become a judge, maybe I'll appear before you."

"Thank you." *Were those tears in his eyes?*

The bailiff asked all the parties to take their places, the jury was already in the box. Judge Celli came out of his chambers and addressed the jury, telling them that the case had been resolved, thanked them for their service, and excused them. He turned to the attorneys and said, "For the record, the District Attorney's Office filed dismissals, with prejudice, this morning. You're all free to go." Then he looked at the defendants, "You are lucky young men. I *never* want to see you again in my court. Please remember that a young woman, a young mother, is dead. You'll have to carry that for the rest of your lives." The boys were taken back to be released.

Judge Celli asked Devin to approach the bench. He said, "I don't like the outcome, but I would like shake your hand. You are one hell of a lawyer."

Devin turned and walked out of the courtroom to be greeted by Eric's parents. He told them to wait a few minutes, Eric would be out. They could take him home.

Somehow the press got wind of the event and when Devin opened the LA times the following morning there was his picture with Eric's smiling parents and a young, humble Marine.

41

Devin took a well-earned break after the Young case. Two weeks in Cancun, soaking up the sun with his wife and kids, downing his share of margaritas, did the trick. He did a lot of thinking and soul-searching and realized that he no longer felt welcome in Ventura. If that was true, he thought to himself, I'm not going to take another case there for a while no matter what the circumstances.

He loved doing his job, but he had an extreme dislike for corrupt law enforcement. The way he saw it, they already had a great advantage over the citizenry. There was no place for lying and cheating, especially not to the people you should be serving and protecting, right? He was grateful that there were watchdog organizations out there to expose them. He was starting to have a whole new appreciation for them.

About a week after his return from vacation, he received a telephone call from Judge Celli. Devin was shocked to hear his voice, but responded with a smile. "To what do I owe the pleasure of your phone call?"

The judge replied, "I want you to know that I have recommended you to our Governor, James Bailey, to head up a new commission sponsored by the California Supreme Court. Their charge is to monitor and review police and prosecutor misconduct. There have been too many incidents of innocent people being convicted and California wants to take the lead in this area. The Innocence Projects in various states, including California, unfortunately, have uncovered many injustices. The Supreme Court felt it was time for the courts to get into the act of cleaning up its own house. I hope you have an interest in righting wrongs."

"I don't know what to say, Your Honor. I've never been on the other side, I don't know if I have the ability to handle something like you are asking me to do. I'm really bad at taking orders from anyone except, maybe my wife?"

Celli laughed and said, "You're going to get a call from the Governor, please take it. They are really earnest."

For once, Devin was at a loss for words. "I'm flattered by your call. I'm not sure I'm worthy of your recommendation, but I'm honored.

"You know you are. You're the champion for the little guy and these days, there aren't many of those."

After Devin hung up he sat in his office in silence, his stomach churning. He kept the call to himself, even from his wife. When the Governor's call came in, everyone heard about it within seconds. Michelle had blurted it out all over the office. Devin explained that it was really nothing. They didn't believe him. They thought he was getting an award or something. When he went home that night, he told his wife. She thought it was great, heading up a public commission to wipe out corruption in the court system. *Devin was still not sure that he was the right candidate.*

In the following days, he flew up to Sacramento and had a four-hour meeting with Governor Bailey and the head of the State Senate and the Chief Justice of the California Supreme Court. It blew him away to find they were just regular people under their official armor, he felt surprisingly comfortable in their company.

They convinced him that he was their choice for the job and assured him that he would have total autonomy over the commission. His only obligation was to file semi-annual reports to the Governor's office. They offered a generous budget and he could select his own staff of attorneys and investigators and he would have the power of the Supreme Court over the issuance of subpoenas. They made clear that they required a commitment from him for three years and would receive a base salary of $250,000, plus expenses. The Governor acknowledged that it would be a big pay cut for him, but the rewards of cleaning up the corruption would be worth it.

The Governor shook hands and laughed, saying, "Who knows? One day you could write a book about all this and go on a lecture tour and make millions." Devin was hooked.

He returned to LA and called an office meeting to tell them the news. They were all stunned but happy for him. He asked Michelle, Ted and Ray to join him in his new venture. He knew it would be a serious conflict of interest to take any criminal cases while he served on the commission, so they needed to help him there, instead. All they wanted to know was how soon they could pack?

He went to his office and closed the door. He swiveled his chair around and took a long, peaceful look at his 'window to the world' ... a long, last look. Then he made the phone call he most enjoyed.

He called Ken Riley and asked him to join the group. "One day, when this is all done, you'll be getting a call offering your judgeship..."

Life is one never-ending adventure, he mused.

www.ingramcontent.com/pod-product-compliance
Lightning Source LLC
Chambersburg PA
CBHW020626220526
45464CB00001B/36